18 Molière: L'Ecole des femmes *and* Le Misanthrope

Critical Guides to French Texts

**EDITED BY ROGER LITTLE, WOLFGANG VAN EMDEN,
DAVID WILLIAMS**

MOLIÈRE

L'Ecole des femmes *and*
Le Misanthrope

J. H. Broome
Emeritus Professor of French
University of Keele

Grant & Cutler Ltd
1993

© Grant & Cutler Ltd
   1993
ISBN 0 7293 0361 6

First edition 1982

Reprinted with corrections 1993

I.S.B.N 84-499-5711-7

DEPÓSITO LEGAL: V. 2.949 - 1993

Printed in Spain by
Artes Gráficas Soler, S. A. - La Olivereta, 28 - 46018 Valencia
for

GRANT & CUTLER LTD
55-57 GREAT MARLBOROUGH STREET, LONDON WIV 2AY

Contents

Contents

Note

REFERENCES given parenthetically in the text of this volume are, for the most part, directly to the Molière texts, with the standard verse-numbering to be found in the Classiques Larousse editions. Where the reference is to secondary literature, it takes the form of an italicized numeral or numerals related to the number of the item/s in the bibliography, with specific page numbers where this is appropriate.

Introduction

France's greatest comic playwright left to posterity more than thirty works covering the entire range of the genre as it was conceived in the seventeenth century and, indeed, extending a long way beyond it, in the opinion of most critics. Of these works about a third can be said to have achieved the status of true classics, with a timeless appeal transcending the tastes, conventions and values of their age and even, perhaps, the initial conceptions and conscious intentions of the author himself, who would doubtless have derived wry amusement from the erudite commentaries and essays of interpretation which they have attracted to themselves. Many of his entertainments can, therefore, be enjoyed without much knowledge of the precise historical circumstances in which they were composed; but it is nevertheless hardly possible to set individual plays in proper perspective without some reference to his career.

He was born Jean-Baptiste Poquelin in 1622, son of a Parisian upholsterer Jean Poquelin, a man of sufficient standing to hold a court-appointment as *Tapissier ordinaire de la maison du Roi*. With this solid middle-class commercial background he had the benefit of a good education, first at the Collège de Clermont and later at Orleans, where he qualified in law, though apparently without much enthusiasm. On the other hand he is known to have interested himself in philosophy (*1*, p. 208; *38*, pp. 18-19; *40*, p. 10), and to have had close and lasting contacts with advanced freethinking circles; and there is no reason to think of him as culturally inferior to great contemporaries such as Corneille or Racine, or indifferent to the intellectual life of the time.

By 1643 he had abandoned any thought of practising law or following in the family business, and committed himself instead to the uncertain life of the stage, largely as a result of his association with the actress Madeleine Béjart who, with her relatives, was to play a continuing part in his affairs. Together with this family and one or two other actors he had a stake in a small theatrical venture calling itself *l'Illustre Théâtre* which, however, foundered in 1645 after a precarious existence in Rouen and Paris. The most illustrious thing connected with it is, indeed, the stage-name of Molière, adopted in 1644 in deference to custom, or to spare his family embarrassment. The name itself – borne previously by the *libertin* writer Molière d'Essertines – is relatable to several villages, but according to his early biographer Grimarest, he never gave reasons for choosing it (*24*, p. 26).

In consequence of the company's failure, Molière was held for debt in the Châtelet prison; but on his release confirmed his devotion to the stage by departing to tour the provinces for thirteen years with a reconstituted troupe, of which he became in effect manager in 1650. These years were spent in the south and south-west of France, with the patronage first of the Duc d'Epernon and later of the Prince de Conti, until his defection in 1657 following a religious conversion. Most of the company's movements have been traced (*1*, pp. 215-220), but the effect of these wanderings on Molière remains a subject for speculation. There is, however, no doubt that they gave him a rich stock of experience and observation; and that to his grasp of the fundamentals of human nature they added that knowledge of the infinite variety of behaviour-patterns – linguistic as well as moral or social – which confers on his writings a considerable documentary value. It was during this period too that Molière turned playwright, beginning with farces, known now mainly as titles, although some of the material was to be used again in later works. The only surviving examples, for which he is believed to have been at least partly responsible, are *La Jalousie du Barbouillé* and *Le Médecin Volant,* neither of them printed until 1819. Although trivial in themselves, they are noteworthy as showing respectively the influence of the native French farce-tradition and that of the Italian *Commedia dell'arte* (*42*, pp. 83-88). His earliest significant literary comedy, *L'Etourdi,* was performed at Lyons, probably in 1655, and was followed soon afterwards by *Le Dépit Amoureux.* These were both full-scale situation-comedies relying mainly on the plots for entertainment-value, and hence somewhat lacking in depth or psychological interest; but they were well-received and provided a basis for success when the company returned in 1658 to try its luck again in Paris.

This time royal patronage, first by the king's brother and then by the young Louis XIV himself, ensured that the disaster of *L'Illustre Théâtre* would not be repeated. By October of that year the company was installed in the Petit-Bourbon theatre with a mixed repertory including tragedies of Corneille; and a year later Molière achieved his first truly important success with *Les Précieuses Ridicules,* the celebrated satire of the contemporary fad of pretentious over-refinement of manners and speech, and the abundant literature – notably the works of Mlle de Scudéry – in which it was manifested. With its flimsy story of two silly girls duped by a pair of masquerading valets this was ostensibly little more than a traditional farce, and as a one-act play could hardly provide a formal model for the later master-pieces; but it remains a landmark simply because of Molière's effective use of farce as a polemical medium, expressing a more or less serious view of a topical issue. Its mockery of an inferior form of literature provides an interesting precedent for later works, including *Le Misanthrope*; and, within its obvious limitations, it offers other examples of what can now be seen as standard Molière features: satire of obsessive and idiosyncratic behaviour; a strong but simple situation involving dupes and rogues; deception and self-deception; criticism of unnatural arti-fice; and also, no doubt, a hint of the cruelty which is perhaps inherent in all ridicule, although not always recog-nized by Molière's devotees. In so far as it appears to present and attack a burlesque form of preciosity rather than the real thing, it also has about it that air of ambiguity which has occasioned much of the argument surrounding Molière's greater plays.

The year 1660 produced only the one-act *Sganarelle ou le Cocu Imaginaire* which, although successful, is note-worthy mainly as an indication that the buffooneries of basic farce were likely to remain as part of Molière's stock-in-trade as a professional entertainer. A certain re-orientation of his career was, however, confirmed at this time by his resumption, following his brother's death, of the family's court-appointment: a gesture towards the powerful political establishment which was itself about to be strengthened in 1661 by Louis XIV's assumption of personal power.

In that year, his company having been moved to the Palais-Royal, Molière presented three works which, though varying in form and fortune, all show him feeling his way towards greater things and still learning by experience. *Don Garcie de Navarre,* a play written some time earlier, is not a true comedy at all, but a "heroic" comedy, and it is important for two reasons: first because its total failure cured its author of any hankering he may have had for tragedy, or particular forms of "seriousness" which ran counter to his true bent; and secondly because its theme of jealousy, and even certain passages of the actual text, remained to be exploited again in *Le Misanthrope,* when he had discovered how serious elements could be genuinely integrated with a comic vision.

In contrast to *Don Garcie de Navarre, L'Ecole des Maris,* which analyses the attitudes of two brothers in their relations with two girls, was a success; and although, as a three-act play, it does not quite qualify as a *grande comédie,* it ranks as an obvious precursor of *L'Ecole des Femmes,* not by virtue of its actual title or plot but by the new mastery of true psychological analysis which it displays, and the character of Sganarelle, the unsympathetic and domineering male who is in some respects a model for Arnolphe (*6,* Pt. III, Vol. 1, pp. 229-238). The themes of marital relationships and the criticism of unnatural inflexibility and tyrannical possess-iveness transcend the artifice of the actual situation, and show clearly that Molière was now poised to make a decisive step and confer upon comedy a dignity of subject-matter, a depth of characterisation and a moral significance which it had not previously displayed. At the same time Molière's potential and basic function as a pure entertainer (and, indeed, as a court-entertainer) were confirmed yet again by the third play of 1661, *Les Fâcheux*, an episodic work or *pièce à tiroirs*, and the first of his hybrid *comédies-ballets*, which presents in review-style a series of sketches of socially irritating or dissonant characters. It was performed as a royal entertainment organized at Vaux by the minister Fouquet. The occasion did not save Fouquet from his impending down-fall, but it gained for the playwright an increased measure of royal approval, and understandably, since it marks an advance in satirical portraiture and comedy of manners, which are prominent features of later plays, including *Le Misanthrope*. In short, the activities of 1661, successful or otherwise, gave notable impetus to the development of Molière's technical skills; and if he still needed profound and significant personal experience to bring his gifts to maturity, this may well have been provided to some extent by his marriage in February 1662 to Armande Béjart, the young sister (or according to some accounts, daughter) of his long-standing associate Madeleine.

Because of the disparity in ages, the part played by her in his career, as wife and actress, has been the subject of much inconclusive speculation (*1*, pp. 229-231; *40*, pp. 55-67). If, as seems probable, she was unfaithful to him, he was philosophical enough to live with the fact; but the marriage probably does have some bearing on both *L'Ecole des Femmes* and *Le Misanthrope*, since the principal relationships and conflicts depicted therein include, among various factors, differences of age or temperament; and the role of Célimène, the coquette of *Le Misanthrope*, was created by Armande, playing to Molière's Alceste. The plays are not autobiographical, but it is reasonable to ascribe in part to Molière's marital experience the deepening of psychological insight and the close analysis of feeling which are to be found beneath the comic surface.

The presentation of *L'Ecole des Femmes* on December 26 1662 was a triumph, perhaps the greatest in Molière's life. It marked the advent of a new force in the French theatre, previously dominated by Corneille; and it confirmed the great potential of his skills without, however, being quite like anything that he had previously written. The play ran throughout the spring of 1663, being performed in the Louvre as well as in the ordinary theatre. Louis XIV was clearly amused by it, and his approval took the tangible form of a pension, and the rather more important intangible form of continuing patronage and protection. It has sometimes been felt that this may have been a disadvantage in the sense that it led Molière subsequently to expend on relatively trivial spectacles energy which might have been more profitably devoted to the production of "straight" dramatic masterpieces. There may be some truth in this, but there is no sign that Molière himself saw it that way; and in any case, without such powerful protection, his independence of mind and critical vigour could well have exposed him to disaster or not found expression at all. As it was, his subsequent career was to be surrounded by controversy and conflict, notably with representatives of religion whose susceptibilities he offended on various occasions, and most of all by his *Tartuffe,* ostensibly directed against religious hypocrisy but seen by many, at the time and since, as an attack upon religion itself. Even with his exalted patronage he had to struggle for five years, from 1664 to 1669, before being authorized to present the play in the full and surviving five-act version; and the affair remains as a remarkable example of the tribulations and persistence of a critical mind caught up in the politics of an authoritarian age. These famous and prolonged controversies began, however, with *L'Ecole des Femmes,* which despite its popular success was greeted also with fierce criticism as an affront to morality and literary proprieties alike. And it is to the ensuing *"querelle de l'Ecole des Femmes"* that we owe one of the happiest examples of theatrical polemic (*1,* pp. 286-293).

In his one-act *Critique de l'Ecole des Femmes* Molière went on to the offensive, dramatising the arguments and caricaturing what he saw as the mindlessness, prejudice and absurdity of his opponents, though providing for himself at the same time strong defensive positions of reason and good sense. Knowledge of the *Critique* may not be essential for the appreciation of *L'Ecole des Femmes* itself; but it remains as the most concise and effective expression of his working principles, and it ensured that the power of laughter would continue to be exercised on Molière's side.

The principles themselves can, of course, be related to "classical" doctrine and attitudes generally; but of the many excellent points made in this fine satire three merit particular emphasis in the present context. The first is his famous proclamation that ultimately the only rule that really matters is that of pleasing the public. The second is his differentiation between tragedy and comedy, and the linking of comedy with everyday life and natural truth in the statement: "Lorsque vous peignez des héros vous faites ce que vous voulez ..... mais lorsque vous peignez les hommes il faut peindre d'après nature; et vous n'avez rien fait si vous n'y faites reconnaître les gens de votre siècle." This assertion leads us towards some particularly interesting aspects of his major characterisations, and the same is true of a third affirmation to the effect that "il n'est pas incompatible qu'une personne soit ridicule en de certaines choses et honnête homme en d'autres." This relates immediately to Arnolphe in *L'Ecole des Femmes,* but it is much more important for our appreciation of the complexities of Alceste in *Le Misanthrope.*

The *Critique de l'Ecole des Femmes* is, therefore, a notable statement of doctrine, but differentiated from many such statements in its satirical edge, its dramatic form and its personification of ideas. This personalised polemic was, moreover, reinforced in a second playlet, *L'Impromptu de Versailles,* which, as it were, took the audience backstage and presented Molière and his company in their own characters – a blending of the real and the theatrical which is sufficient answer to any who may feel inclined to cast doubt on his originality.

After indulging in these pleasurable polemics Molière had to experience the darker side of life, with the death of his first child, before resuming more positive work; and even then it was to produce, not major comedies, but material for court-entertainments. In 1664 *Le Mariage Forcé,* inspired by Rabelais, was given as a three-act *Comédie-Ballet* before being reduced to a one-act play for the theatre proper; and in May of the same year his *Princesse d'Elide* formed part of the splendid three-day spectacle given by the king at Versailles as *Les Plaisirs de l'Ile Enchantée.* As a mixture of pastoral and fantasy, Molière's contribution is now of interest mainly as exemplifying the intense pressure to which he was too often subjected in his multiple role as actor-manager-author. In this instance shortage of time compelled him to complete in prose a work begun in verse: a fact worth remembering whenever he is thought to have lapsed from the highest standards of craftsmanship, or judged to have written better prose than verse.

Fortunately, his labours were not restricted to these relatively ephemeral productions, for 1664 also brought the first three-act version of *Tartuffe,* the performance of which was, however, promptly forbidden in Paris. So began the most difficult phase of his career, during which his resilience was to be severely tested (*27,* pp. 132-134). In the first place, his company's programme was badly disrupted by the prohibition, and further compromised by the death of one of his leading actors, Du Parc, in November 1664; and in the same month he suffered the death of another child. In these circumstances he was hard put to it to obey the theatre's basic precept that the show – or some sort of show – must go on. *Le Misanthrope,* on which he was working, was not yet in a presentable state, so he cast around for material suitable for rapid exploitation. It turned out to be the story of Don Juan, which had already been dramatised in France as well as in Spain and Italy; and his company staged *Dom Juan ou le Festin de Pierre* as a stopgap, on February 15 1665. After fifteen performances this too was withdrawn, since its philosophical content and above all its portrayal of a *grand seigneur méchant homme* were only too clearly related to the *Tartuffe* controversy. Although he obtained a privilege, Molière did not publish it himself, and it has been left to later generations to restore an authentic text to its rightful place in the canon of his works, and to modern critics to argue over its significance.

Dom Juan is, in fact, his most extraordinary play, and one which signals an important development of the Don Juan theme in European literature. It is also a highly episodic work, written apparently in total defiance of the formal conventions of the time; and although some of its peculiarities are attributable to the source-material (including a supernatural element), or to rapid improvisation, it has nevertheless a direct bearing on our appreciation of his other major works, by reason of its mingling of the comic and the serious, and above all the ambiguity of its central characterisations, which generate considerable doubt as to Molière's personal attitudes.

The term ambiguity is applicable not only to the play itself, but to the circumstances in which it was dropped from the repertory. This was certainly the result of discreet pressure from above; but it is significant that shortly afterwards Molière received an increased pension, and his company was given formal recognition as the *Troupe du Roi* – an important step leading to the formation of what has become the *Comédie Française*. In response to this accolade, Molière had once more to play the role of court-entertainer, and the immediate result was *L'Amour Médecin*. This is a lightweight piece containing nevertheless one of the best of his famous caricatures of the medical profession; and it is noteworthy also for a short preface, one sentence of which should be in the mind of everybody who is required to "study" him.

> On sait bien que les comédies ne sont faites que pour être jouées; et je ne conseille de lire celle-ci qu'aux personnes qui ont des yeux pour découvrir dans la lecture tout le jeu du théâtre.

L'Amour Médecin took no more than five days to produce, and so did not distract Molière from what was now his main preoccupation. A new masterpiece was in the making, and on

June 4 1666 there took place the first performance of *Le Misanthrope*.

As happens not infrequently, this outstanding work had a lukewarm reception, and the enthusiasm of a discerning minority (which included the critic Boileau) could not compensate for the indifference of a general public wanting for its money more action and visible drama than is likely to be generated by any salon-comedy. Whatever private disappointment Molière may have felt over its relatively modest run, it is typical of the man (and highly instructive for his commentators) that he should have followed it two months later with the primitive and joyous farce of *Le Médecin Malgré Lui*, before turning to a series of the minor, conventional and less significant entertainments which seem to have been more or less forced on him in his semi-privileged position. A further attempt to establish *Tartuffe* in the repertory failed in 1667 after a single performance, but his persistence was rewarded in 1669, when opposition to the play was finally overcome (*27*, pp. 33-131).

During the last five years of his career more favourable circumstances allowed the production of eleven more works, mostly comedies of high quality except for the rather odd *tragédie-ballet Psyché*, written in collaboration with the ageing Corneille and the composer Lully. There was, however, a setback in 1672 in that Lully then obtained a virtual monopoly for productions requiring more than four musicians. This has been interpreted as a sign that the king's support was on the wane; but Molière's disappointment is a reminder that he was never devoted exclusively to the production of straight plays with a message, but was more than willing, as a public entertainer, to follow the fashions, which now included opera (*1*, pp. 196-7).

The works which have genuinely survived from this last and fertile period include *Amphitryon*, perhaps the most charming of his situation-comedies; his best, if not immediately successful farce *Les Fourberies de Scapin; George Dandin*, with its rather sombre view of marital relations; and four plays containing some of his most popular character-studies. Of these, *L'Avare* and *Les Femmes Savantes* are straight comedies, but *Le Bourgeois Gentilhomme* and *Le Malade Imaginaire* both include a spectacular element of comic ballet as sheer gratuitous fun. It was, nevertheless, while playing the title-role of the Hypochondriac on 17 February 1673 that Molière was struck down and carried off to a swift death and a grudgingly-granted Christian burial – a melancholy yet appropriately ironic end, which his enemies could no doubt regard as a divine judgment but which his admirers have preferred to see as an exemplary and honourable death in harness.

Such, in outline, was Molière's career, and it does not require much contemplation to draw from it a few general conclusions which are worth bearing in mind as we examine particular works or aspects of his art. The first is that he was a man dedicated primarily and essentially to what is nowadays called show-business: a man of the boards rather than the study; a *manager* with an eye on the box-office; a *producer,* with a producer's understanding of the *optique du théâtre,* not too much concern with "naturalism", and a feel for audience-reactions at different levels; and a practising clown and actor, using mime as much as verbal communication, and frequently playing the leading roles in what were obviously conceived as *pièces à vedette* – in short, a total and serious professional with a high sense of the dignity of his chosen work.

Secondly, he had a literary culture, intellectual depth and critical intelligence of a quality not always found in entertainers but comparable with those of the great tragic playwrights of the time, with whose works there are, in fact, some important points of contact.

Thirdly, Molière was not a snob, intellectually or socially; and although critics have claimed to detect a "class" angle in his work (without agreeing as to which class), he evidently saw his function as the amusement of all comers, whether groundlings, or patrons or the *honnêtes gens* of the time. Consequently he can be seen picking his way delicately between realism and fantasy, and the result is a body of work so varied that it cannot be adequately represented by one or two plays. Those to be examined in the following pages have been selected to show two of the most interesting stages in his development. *L'Ecole des Femmes* illustrates the emergence of comedy from a background of farce, to provoke thought as well as laughter; and *Le Misanthrope* the highest point of refinement and subtlety to which he brought his chosen genre.

1

L'Ecole des Femmes:
Sources and Structure

THE success of *L'Ecole des Femmes* from its first performance on 26 December 1662 is an indication of genuine merit which has been more than confirmed by its standing in the repertory for more than three centuries; but it must be acknowledged that initially it was also a *succès de scandale*. The war of pamphlets and parodies which it unleashed involved not only lesser writers or disgruntled rivals such as Boursault or Montfleury, but the major figures of Pierre and Thomas Corneille; and the range of the attacks included serious moral condemnation from feminists and the more puritanical religious groups as well as trivial technical objections (*6,* Pt. III, Vol. I, pp. 265-268). Among the criticisms, the one requiring immediate consideration is the charge of plagiarism, because the play can indeed be related to various earlier works, two of which were rapidly noted by the young writer Donneau de Visé as possible sources of broad inspiration.

The first is Scarron's *La Précaution Inutile,* a story known to Molière and itself based on a Spanish original by María de Zayas. It tells of the misadventure of a nobleman whose betrothed has a daughter by another man, but who takes the child and, from the age of four, has her educated in a convent, removed from worldly temptations and supervised otherwise only by unintelligent servants. In this version the girl's protector, after various adventures, returns to marry her, taking care to supplement his earlier measures with admonitions as to the conduct appropriate to the married state. Despite these safeguards the *ingénue* wife is seduced; and by naïvely revealing all to her accident-prone husband demonstrates that ignorance is no guarantee of virtue – a piece of "instruction" which reappears of course as one of Molière's themes.

The second reference by Donneau de Visé is to *Le Piacevoli Notti,* a collection of tales published in 1550 by the rather earthy Italian writer Straparola, in one of which a prince makes indiscreet revelations about his love, not realising that the recipient of his confidences is his lady's husband. Since this too was circulating in a translation, it could conceivably have suggested the main development of situation-comedy in *L'Ecole des Femmes,* though this remains conjectural.

Apart from these hypothetical sources and some obvious elements of thematic continuity with Molière's own *Ecole des Maris,* there are echoes of other writers including Plautus, Terence, Rabelais, Lope de Vega and Corneille (*6,* Pt. III, Vol. I, pp. 244-247); but it is doubtful whether they offered him much in the way of general inspiration that he would not have taken almost automatically from the stock situations and characters of the farce-tradition, such as the conflict between young lovers and some obstacle-character, of whom his Arnolphe is but one of innumerable variants.

Taken together, however, the evidence and the conjectures confirm that the play is partly derivative, and thus raise general questions about Molière's "originality". The short answer to them is that his borrowings are of little consequence, since he was writing at a time when art tended to be judged normatively as a performance within a tradition, and originality was deemed to be manifested, as Pascal put it, in "placing the ball" rather than in using a new ball. What really matters, therefore, is the skill with which he has adapted and supplemented the subject-matter to provide an effective theatrical entertainment and transform a loose narrative into a tight drama.

Many of the changes are straightforward and predictable: for example, the substitution of a middle-class setting, the actual suppression of much of the narrative, or the bringing into personal contact of rivals who in Scarron's version do not meet at all. Less predictable, perhaps, but reflecting the tendency to emphasize psychological content rather than physical incidents, which had been visible in the French theatre since the emergence of Corneille, is Molière's decision to present much of his action not directly, but through the mediating device of the *récit*. To do this so extensively may have been something of a gamble, but if so, it has certainly succeeded brilliantly.

If Scarron's tale is indeed the major source, one problem it posed for Molière is that of the moral tone. This he has evidently refined, if only by rejecting marriage as a situation in the play and so doing away with any actual seduction or adultery. As a concession to *bienséance* this is worth noting in view of the qualms which his critics professed to feel on the subject of impropriety, and notably over the famous and equivocal "le" in Act II, 5; but it is doubtful whether decorum was Molière's real concern. More to the point is the fact that potential situations may be more exploitable than actual ones for both comic and dramatic purposes, and in this case provide the logical accompaniment to Arnolphe's morbid fear of being cuckolded.

A more technical problem is posed by the adaptation of the story to the system of dramatic unities, to which Molière obviously attached no sanctity, but which he was prepared to observe as far as possible. In this case he has produced a more or less unified action and conformed to the unity of place, although the setting of a public square strains probability. In the matter of timing, his problem is much the same as that which confronted the contemporary tragic playwrights in their efforts to extract tightly-knit dramatic actions from the long-running sagas of antiquity. The story itself may be quite short, but its time-scale is longer than would normally be expected in a comedy. It is therefore very important to choose the right point at which to cut into the story (as Horace observed many centuries earlier in the *Ars Poetica*); and it is interesting to note that Molière has here done what Racine was to do a few years later in his tragedies – i.e. begun his stage action at a point as close as possible to the end of the story. Just as a typical Racinian play can be conceived, in a sense, as "all dénouement", in which a long-prepared explosion of passion is, as it were, recorded in slow motion, so *L'Ecole des Femmes* details the climactic and catastrophic events of a few hours which nullify the endeavours and preoccupations of twenty years, with the preliminaries recalled in a brief exposition and a few subsequent allusions.

Paradoxically, however, it is the solution to this problem which actually poses another; for Molière now has to expand his catastrophe in such a way as to fill five acts with viable and sustained comedy. To achieve this he has first done the obvious thing and extended the range or multiplied the nuances of psychological analysis (albeit at the cost of some long speeches which modern audiences could bear to see shortened); but he has also looked for a self-renewing joke-situation capable of being developed with variations. He may or may not have found it in Straparola, but he has certainly seized upon the possibility of a *series* of indiscreet revelations made under a misapprehension as to identity, using repetition, and above all repeated frustration, to heighten both dramatic tension and amusement. This is a well-tested technique of farce which, because of its efficacy, has been constantly revived in more modern forms of gratuitous amusement such as those of the music-hall or silent film-comedy; and it is at that level that Molière's exploitation of his source-material must first be appreciated.

None of this explains, however, why *L'Ecole des Femmes* is also a *grande comédie*; and to gain some insight into this further question it is worth looking again at the probable relationship to Scarron's *Précaution Inutile*. On doing so, one discovers, surprisingly, that for background purposes Molière has, in a sense, actually lengthened the time-scale. Whereas the adventure of Scarron's Don Pedro begins as a reaction to a concrete situation on the part of a man already committed in principle to marriage, Molière's Arnolphe has been studying marriage as a condescending bachelor and spectator for at least seven years, before becoming personally involved at all. This means that his whole approach to the question is in the first instance theoretical, and that we are likely to find in Molière's version not just a farcical entertainment or a cruelly funny story, but a play going much more deeply into motives and inhibitions to produce a genuine psychological study, with important moral and even philosophical implications. This is what begins to make possible the creation of that profound "character-comedy" which gives him his special place in the spectrum of drama; and this is the point, therefore, at which we can turn from the alleged sources to concentrate further on his transformation of the subject.

One of the most important things he has done is to enrich the whole thematic basis: for example, by adding to the lesson on ignorance and virtue which is already in *La Précaution Inutile* another simple "moral", encapsulated in the *vers-maxime*

> ... qui rit d'autrui
> Doit craindre qu'en revanche on rie aussi de lui.
>
> (vv. 45-46)

More important than this, needless to say, is the "school" of the title, which in its true sense turns out to be love. Beyond this, however, is another theme, suggested rather than formally stated, which is, simply, man's desire for a perfect wife. Now the obvious comment on this theme is that nothing could be less novel, and hence more universal in its import or more capable of eliciting a ready response in the theatre. But nothing could be more dangerously simplistic (or more characteristic of the entire history of human folly) than the "philosophy" which Arnolphe brings to the pursuit of his ideal; for, having pondered for years on the possible infelicities of marriage and the statistics of cuckoldry (as distorted, no doubt, by his own insecure and prurient mind), he decides, in effect, to avoid the risks of marital infidelity by creating his own perfect mate. The God-like nature of this do-it-yourself enterprise is close enough to the *hubris* of the ancients to explain at once why the play can be seen ultimately not simply as a farce, or for that matter as a *grande comédie,* but also as a kind of burlesque tragedy with – as some have uneasily felt – more than a hint of the real thing. In its absurdity it has all the comic potential associated with disproportion between energy expended and result achieved, or incongruity of ends and means; but it also holds the prospect of real suffering if any genuine emotion is allowed in, and if the scheme fails, as no doubt it must.

The probability of the failure of such radical thinking derives, of course, from the impossibility of establishing the right conditions, and from a variety of brute, intractable realities which are either manifested in the play or are at least deducible from the expository discussion between Arnolphe and his friend Chrysalde. First, since Arnolphe is not God, but an unusually insecure bachelor with limited scope for practical action, he cannot create literally *ex nihilo* but must start with human, and specifically female nature in its simplest accessible state, here represented by the naïve mind of the four-year-old Agnès, a girl he has adopted from a poor peasant background. Ostensibly she is an orphan, but it will be revealed ultimately that she is the offspring of Chrysalde's sister and fruit of a secret marriage. On comparing her with other children, he has convinced himself, in deadly earnest, that she truly represents a *bonté naturelle* – a point which is, incidentally, of quite serious philosophical interest when contrasted with the insistence on the taint of Original Sin, so prevalent in the seventeenth century and seen, for example, in the theology of Bossuet, or the disenchanted moralising of La Rochefoucauld or Pascal.

Arnolphe's next step is, therefore, to arrange for a long process of mainly negative conditioning, aimed at insulating the child from corrupt society and so producing a wife whose morality is to be reduced to submissiveness and whose activities are to be restricted to the acquisition of simple domestic skills. But since he cannot, for social and other reasons, directly execute the scheme himself, he has had to accept once more the second-best solution and put her into a convent, insisting nevertheless that the regime be more restrictive than is normal (I, 1, vv. 137-8), and regretting – with reason – that she should even be taught to write, although he cannot prevent it (III, 4, vv. 946-7). After removing her in due course from the convent, Arnolphe has attempted to maintain the insulation of Agnès by installing her in a separate house, with (as in Scarron's tale) a minimal human presence in the shape of the servants Alain and Georgette, whose peasant stupidity – lovingly played for laughs as part of the *jeu du théâtre* – is, again, the best available substitute for the absolute innocence which a more normal social environment cannot provide. As for his own relationship with the girl until she reaches marriageable age, when the play actually begins, this too is situated on a plane of unreality by his adoption of a second identity under the pretentious name of Monsieur de la Souche. This "debaptising" of Arnolphe is Molière's essential plot invention, and one which merits special attention.

Since the literal meaning of *souche* is a tree-stump (and in this play specifically a rotten one), the genealogical connotations of the name belong no doubt to the realm of pure farce, but the obsession with the aristocratic *particule* does not. On the one hand it relates to the real world of contemporary snobbery which was to be satirized by Molière on various occasions, and notably in *Le Bourgeois Gentilhomme;* but it also returns again to the plane of perverted idealism in its comic-heroic evocation of a feudal past, with Arnolphe in the role of *seigneur*. It is characteristic of the complex ironies and multi-dimensional quality of Molière's comedy at its best that he should have made of Arnolphe's dual identity, which is in the first instance the primitive device on which the whole plot-mechanism is based, the occasion for a double name-joke, traditional in that Arnolphe is a legendary "patron" of cuckolds, and topical in that "Monsieur de la Souche" has both an independent life as social satire and a special relevance to a particular psychological study. It must be added, as a further indication of the totality of Molière's artistic conception, that the idea of obscured identity, both as invented plot-device and as theme, will reappear in relation to Agnès herself, the assertion of whose true identity, in the civil and the psychological sense alike, is an essential part of the dénouement, and indeed of the morality of the play.

Given these dispositions by Arnolphe, which represent his challenge to "normal" life as he sees it, all that Molière now needs, to bring us to the threshold of a stage drama, is to ensure that the curtain will rise at the moment of truth, when the theory is to be put to the test; and, in order to have an actual play as distinct from the study of a relationship, to complete a triangle with the character who will break Agnès's isolation and ensure the survival of her true instinctive nature and individual personality, despite the previous conditioning. This character is Horace, at first generously welcomed by Arnolphe as the son of an old friend, but destined, as the play evolves, to become the symbol of all that he fears. The other figures in the play are all minor ones, serving to provide a perspective of normality, or to complete the mechanism of the arbitrary plot. The most interesting of these, as will be seen later, is Chrysalde. He has at least some individuality, in comparison with which his brother-in-law Enrique, and Horace's father Oronte are two-dimensional figures making a late entrance to provide a happy ending for Agnès and Horace – a "miracle" which is nevertheless carefully hinted at in the play's exposition. For, as a single pull unravels the knot of the action, it is disclosed that Enrique is the true but long-lost father of Agnès, re-appearing providentially with wealth acquired during fourteen years in America, and the precise intention of recovering her and marrying her to "the son of Oronte", whom he does not know but who turns out – need it be said? – to be Mr Right after all ....

And lest this final pull be made too soon, a place has been found in Act IV for the episodic character of a Notary, summoned for the abortive marriage-plans of Arnolphe, but whose real function is to fill out the expanded catastrophe, it being one of the merits of the play that the conclusion is retarded to the very limit.

In summary, therefore, Molière's development of his source-material has resulted in a simple basic situation involving only three genuinely significant characters, but turned into a fertile source of extremely funny scenes by Horace's ignorance of the fact that he is repeatedly revealing his measures to rescue Agnès from Monsieur de la Souche to Monsieur de la Souche – in the person of his "friend" Arnolphe. Since this ignorance can be prolonged at will by the author, it can be used to intensify the degree of commitment on both sides of the conflict, to sustain dramatic interest as well as amusement, to cater for the audience's curiosity by the matching of obsessive and well-informed calculation against a combination of two forms of naïvety, and above all, to create a system of comic irony, in which the audience itself is deeply involved through Molière's skilful use of monologues and narrations, which actually become part of the action. In this we can sense not only the competence of the writer, but the remarkable "feel" of the actor-producer.

2
L'Ecole des Femmes:
The Scheme of Characters

From what has been seen so far, it might be assumed that *L'Ecole des Femmes* is essentially a farce-based situation-comedy, technically interesting but orientated to a world of artifice and comic fantasy. If it were no more than that, it would doubtless have achieved immediate success with the public; but its continuing prestige within the canon of Molière's plays suggests that it possesses some high quality of truth distinguishable from the integrity of the play-maker's craft. Since this quality can hardly be attributed to the plot as such, it must lie in the characterisation and the relationship between characters; and this is what Molière had in mind when, replying to his critics in scene 6 of the *Critique de l'Ecole des Femmes,* he differentiated "men" from "heroes" and set up a criterion of realism or "truth to nature" in respect of the characters of comedy. This does not mean that the element of realism has to be developed over the same range in all the characters, any more than all the characters have to be intrinsically comic; but it does suggest that all of them, even the most functional ones, should show recognizably human rather than puppet-faces. If they are examined according to the scale of importance and complexity, it will be seen that this is indeed the case.

The simplest ones are of course those needed purely for the plot, beginning with the father-figures Oronte and Enrique, of whom little need be said other than that they are not comic, but not unrealistic. Unlike many of Molière's fathers, they are not eccentrics; and so far as their brief appearances permit, they express the kind of paternal sentiments which were presumably normal at a time of arranged marriages. Not being markedly authoritarian, they can contribute to the atmosphere of general rejoicing in which the wretched Arnolphe is finally abandoned to his fated isolation.

By comparison with these thin but necessary characters, the Notary seems almost a supernumerary; but the episode in which he figures is genuinely interesting in relation to both comedy and realism. For example, apart from filling time, his encounter with Arnolphe in Act IV, 2, is also intended to provide comic relief, the necessity for which is very remarkable in a work purporting to be a comedy pure and simple. It arises because with the approach of the climax, an element of deep emotion has begun to show itself in the behaviour of Arnolphe; and to an extent which would take us outside the range of comedy altogether if it were not carefully controlled.

The relief provided takes two forms, the first being Molière's use of the comic device of *soliloques simultanés* (vv. 1039-1060) to create a non-dialogue which begins because the two speakers do not see each other physically, but is prolonged because they do not register each other mentally, each being trapped in his own mental world. Secondly, the Notary is, by Molière's criteria, a comic character in his own right, representative of a whole gallery of "professionals" whose jargon-ridden ratiocinations (vv. 1063-1077) set them apart from normal people. The portrait is, no doubt, a caricature, related to a long tradition of satire of the legal profession and animated by Molière's personal distaste; but it is also realistic in so far as it stems from his long study of specialized forms of human behaviour. The Notary is, in fact, as obsessed as Arnolphe, and exemplifies admirably the way in which even minor and apparently stock figures in Molière's plays are individualized and coloured by the general context.

This applies also to Arnolphe's confidant Chrysalde, who is more interesting than he looks because he has a triple function: mechanical, moral and psychological. At the purely mechanical level, he plays his part in both the exposition and the dénouement; at the moral level he voices the common-sense which is the necessary foil to Arnolphe's idiosyncrasy,

and to that extent is, on the face of it, an early representative
of that well-defined body of Molière characters known as
raisonneurs. But he has a more positive role than most of
them by virtue of his particular brand of raillery, which
seems calculated not so much to bring Arnolphe to reason as
to goad him into even greater commitment to his obsession
with cuckoldry and its cure (e.g. IV, 8, vv. 1228-1318). He
thus contributes to the "psychology" of the main character,
but in a way which seems to foreshadow the notorious ambiguity of the character of Philinte in *Le Misanthrope*. Since he
is perpetually reminding Arnolphe of the "fatal" nature of
cuckoldry as something to be borne with stoic resignation,
Chrysalde also contributes to the element of pure burlesque
in the play. Although he can be played with a touch of
buffoonery, particularly in the first scene, he is nevertheless
credible as a reflection of Molière's own encounters with the
great mass of disenchanted humanity; and his curiosity to see
just how far Arnolphe will go is certainly rooted in observed
reality.

With the servants Alain and Georgette, we come to the
last of the minor functional figures, and those who appear to
derive directly from Scarron. The obvious development is
that Molière has worked them up into real French peasant
characters, comparable with his presentation of the lower
orders in many other plays. Again, it must be stressed that he
had been well-placed to observe them; and if their behaviour
is reduced to utterly farcical stupidity, this is mainly because
the ironic system of the plot requires it. In fact, they are not
as stupid as they look, particularly in relation to money; and
the point is well made in the amusing fourth scene of Act IV,
where they give Arnolphe a lesson on the perils of "conditioning" which echoes and parodies at the farce-level a
major philosophical theme of the play (vv. 1117-1130). It is
hardly necessary to add that simply because they *are* servants
they contribute to the "psychology" of Arnolphe by providing for the display of his nastier "seigneurial" characteristics.
Of them, as of the other minor characters, it can be said that
they make a positive contribution to the comedy, and that in
themselves they justify Molière's general claim to "peindre

d'après nature", advanced in scene 6 of the *Critique de l'Ecole des Femmes*.

Of the major figures, the easiest one to assess seems to be Horace; but even in his case it is clear that the subject contains problems as well as opportunities. Traditionally – and almost by definition – the part of the *jeune premier* tends to be ungrateful and unrewarding; and the history of the theatre (and of Molière's own productions) is littered with examples of pleasant but rather wooden young men: lovers whom the world may love, but does not necessarily find very interesting.

In this instance, however, Molière has profited from his earlier experience with the play *L'Etourdi* to provide a better-than-average opportunity for the actor; and La Grange, who created the role, could have had no grounds for complaint as far as the actual comedy is concerned. Horace is at least at the heart of the situation, with possibilities of initiative; and his changes of fortune, alternating with those of Arnolphe, provide a continuing focus for both drama and mainly sympathetic laughter. As the *jeune étourdi* of a situation-comedy he may not provide much scope for elaboration, but it is to Molière's credit that he has been able to infuse some sort of life into him, and thus transform another stock figure into a fairly solid and credible character. It must be understood, however, that his significance in the play derives not just from what he is or does, but from what Arnolphe *thinks* he is. Although he is the son of an old friend, he must inevitably be regarded as a threat, if only because of his spontaneous ardour, contrasting with Arnolphe's forty-two years (although this is not shown to be important to Agnès). It is worth noting that except at their first encounter, and on one subsequent occasion (III, 4, v. 853) where there is an ironic "Seigneur Horace", Arnolphe never uses the young man's name, but refers to him as a "blondin séducteur", "jeune blondin", "blondin funeste" and so on (vv. 596, 645, 722, 1208, 1561). He does so because he is "depersonalising" him (as he would depersonalise Agnès) and reducing him to a representative of the *category* of seducers, which is, apparently, how his obsession leads him to conceive of the entire young male population. Now it may be that Horace really is, to begin with, a potential seducer, not averse to the fleeting enjoyment of a *bonne fortune,* but as the play develops he is confirmed in the character of a decent young man, unwilling to abuse the innocence of his love, and prepared to brave his father's displeasure in order to keep her. Nevertheless he too acquires, at least in the mind of Arnolphe, a kind of secondary identity and a "fixed" status which seems to be the psychological equivalent of the masked personage of the farce tradition. It is, however, a measure of the irony of Molière's scheme that the "corruption" of the world is personified by Arnolphe in a youth whose main characteristics, from the standpoint of normal people, are in fact ingenuousness and good intentions. If Horace is to be categorized at all, it should be as the archetypal rescuer of a damsel in distress – an agreeable young fellow with an eye for a pretty face, and not too quick on the uptake. In this respect, and quite apart from what his treatment tells us about the mind of Arnolphe, he is exactly what the plot requires, and the damsel will inevitably fall in love with him.

As a character, Horace is soundly developed within the limits of his actual role, and is a credible human being. The case of Agnès, however, is not quite so straightforward, because here the plot requires a much greater development, from passivity to activity, and at a speed which has exposed Molière to charges of implausibility. From time to time critical minds have boggled at the rapid transformation of a young female *automate,* first seen as little more than a human sewing-machine, with no outlet for any normal sensibilities other than religious ritual, into a spirited and resourceful young lady, able not only to assert and defend her rights as a person, but to destroy the whole mental world of Arnolphe with a striking combination of ruse and art-lessness. Here, more perhaps than anywhere in the play, the question must arise: is Molière's portrait painted *d'après nature*?

In fact, this question can be partly evaded by anyone who believes that there is an autobiographical element in the work, and that Agnès reflects something of the young

Armande Béjart who had touched Molière's heart as a child, and whom he had married not long before. She probably does, so it can always be argued that at the very least Molière was exceptionally well placed to appreciate with what momentous consequences little girls get bigger every day, and that "nature" must therefore figure largely in the characterisation.

Nevertheless, there is here a genuine critical point, so we should note that in the first instance it is a matter of art, to be judged in relation to the *optique du théâtre*. In this perspective exaggerations and simplifications are permissible; and it must be accepted that the arbitrary elements of both farce and *comédie d'intrigue* which entered into Molière's conception of his play absolve us from the need to worry excessively over the time-factor – the more so since the change in Agnès's behaviour takes about eight days and not the few hours ostensibly dictated by the unity of time. The objection that this is still an unacceptable straining of probabilities can only be met by looking again at both the comic and the psychological factors in the whole situation.

In the first place, the mere fact that thirteen laborious years of conditioning are nullified in a matter of days, whether one or eight, is sufficient indication that Molière is invoking the aid of that great source of comic effect – disproportion. But the disproportion cannot be felt without mental reference to the other side of the situation: i.e. Arnolphe's enormous investment of thought and time. It follows that the quicker the development of Agnès, the more effective is Molière's exposition of the absurdity of Arnolphe's enterprise, which is, after all, his main concern both as moralist and entertainer. It also follows that accusations of unrealistic characterisation based on Agnès seen in isolation are simply misdirected. As a corollary to this, the fact that Agnès responds almost immediately to Horace, in however naïve a way, is relatable to the whole scheme of comic irony; for Arnolphe himself admits (I, 1, vv. 129-130) to having been "inspired" with love for Agnès on seeing her with other children at the age of four. We are dealing here with revelations and wild surmises as to new possibilities,

almost in the sense of *conversion;* and if we accept thirteen
years of preparation and patient expectation as a fair measure
of their impact on Arnolphe, there is no need to cavil at the
speed and intensity of Agnès's own "conversion", also inspired by a new and sudden vision of life's possibilities. Wrong
though it may have seemed to some, the characterisation of
Agnès is artistically and psychologically justifiable, though
this cannot, perhaps, be fully appreciated without reference
to Arnolphe and to the whole drama of their relationship.

The first point to be made about Arnolphe himself is that
in relation both to farce and *comédie d'intrigue* his role, like
that of the young lovers, is in the first instance a conventional
one. As an older man, as an obstacle-figure and as a *Jaloux,*
he has countless forerunners and successors; and the tradition
to which he belongs, and in which Molière had been more or
less immersed and schooled, does not necessarily call for very
detailed characterisation. In that world of fixed-mask figures,
human nature tends to be simplified to black-and-white
terms, and behaviour into mechanical routines which may
indeed bear the stamp of the exaggerated and the grotesque,
but do not involve much subtlety. It is, in short, a kind of
Punch-and-Judy world with a suggestion of violence, in
which characters of this kind elicit a child-like reaction of
mingled amusement and awe; and something of its spirit
certainly survives in *L'Ecole des Femmes.* It is evoked, for
example, in Act II, 2 and 3, with the comic terror of the
servants before the incoherent wrath of the most "hideux
chrétien" which their master has become through the
upsetting of his dream-world (II, 3, v. 417); and in the
exaggerated raillery of Chrysalde; and it was doubtless
savoured as much by Molière the actor as by his audiences.
But he also saw that the traditional and primitive character-
schemes offered scope for a creative enterprise which would
establish contact with the "gens de son siècle" and put comedy on a level equal to, perhaps even superior to, that of
tragedy, by the development of a character at least to
heroic *proportions,* far more satisfying not only to the author
but to the actor in him.

The second and obvious point about Arnolphe is, there-fore, the sheer scale of the role, rarely exceeded in any other of Molière's productions. *L'Ecole des femmes* is the first of Molière's real *pièces à vedette,* in which, except for one short scene in Act II, Arnolphe is on stage from begin-ning to end. His personality must, therefore, become the main focus of attention, and this is impossible unless the "psychology" is widened and deepened far beyond the imme-diate functional requirements of straightforward situation-comedy. This in turn may well open up questions not only as to *what* Arnolphe is, but *why;* and it explains why the char-acter has exercised a fascination and stimulated interpretative arguments of a kind which Molière himself probably never envisaged.

Theoretically the question *what?* should be answerable without much difficulty; the trouble is that it can be answered at different levels, and that different facets of the character are revealed successively as the plot develops. This makes for complexity and even paradox, as can be seen by reference on the one hand to theatrical tradition, and on the other, to Molière's probable source-material. From the first, Arnolphe has inherited the function of obstacle to young love, and is thus antipathetic and fair game for ridicule almost by definition. In relation to the second, however, he can be conceived as a victim of unfortunate circumstances and hence a possible object of sympathy, at least in the abstract. It is this paradox which has provided Molière with scope for the production of a remarkable psychological study, and he has taken full advantage of it.

Some of Arnolphe's characteristics are of course revealed directly in the exposition, and they go some way towards answering the question *why?* From it we learn that he is a well-to-do bourgeois and an ageing bachelor with plenty of social contacts. These include genuine friends such as Chrysalde and Oronte, with whom he deals straightforwardly, preferring sincerity to social affectations; and he is capable of generosity, as in his first reception of Horace (I, 4, vv. 281-2). He is educated and articulate, and normal enough in much of his behaviour to be taken seriously as a human being and not relegated to the ranks of utterly grotesque deviationists. On the other hand it is clear that beneath the surface there are long-standing difficulties and that he is not a truly integrated person. We are not told about his actual sexual experience, if any, although Chrysalde's reference to a "vieux tronc pourri" (I, 1, v. 171) as part of the Monsieur de la Souche joke may be an oblique allusion. We are, however, informed about his little peculiarity, which is enough to set up any psychoanalyst in business. For Arnolphe is a self-appointed recorder of scandals, a connoisseur of seduction and cuckoldry in the abstract, a man in whom a possibly genuine contempt for the *mores* of the time has turned into a sort of moral, if not physical voyeurism, whose appetite grows with what it feeds on. So much so that he is prepared to encourage young Horace in the paths of seduction, until he realises that his own interest is at stake. Sexual scandal is his "plaisir de prince" (I, 4, v. 297); and of all the *manies* exhibited in Molière's character-comedies none is more remarkable than this, or more capable of suggesting that beneath the absurdities there is a whole world of personal and social inadequacies which, potentially, is as much tragic as comic.

Without flirting unduly with unverifiable and anachronistic speculations, we can at least assume that the psychological starting-point of Arnolphe's adventure is some form of social or sexual failure; and most of his behaviour in and before the action of the play can be construed as compensatory in some sense, and mainly as a flight to the ideal, to escape from the intolerable frustrations of his reality and find the *power* and self-esteem which this denies him.

Although the characterisation has an obvious sexual reference, this is not the only focus of interest, for he is depicted as an outsider in a broader sense, and as a wilful individualist and nonconformist. As he says to Chrysalde

> En femme, *comme en tout,* je veux suivre ma mode.
> (I, 1, v. 124)

but the question is: is he an outsider because he is an individualist, or is he an individualist because he is a *de facto* outsider driven, as it were, to make a virtue of necessity for the purpose of self-reassurance? This is a question which is applicable to other plays of Molière, including *Le Misanthrope,* and the second explanation seems to be the more probable. It accounts for the snobbish aspect of "Monsieur de la Souche" as well as the misconceived idealism of the creative effort with Agnès; it explains the power-motive in both, and it explains why he emerges in the course of the play as a *tyrant* and exploiter of the young girl. If the tyrannical tendency and the desire for possession represent a bolstering of the ego due to a sense of inadequacy and non-possession, then this portrait of Arnolphe gives a brilliant expression of it. And it becomes clear why, on the one hand, and in his dealings with Horace in particular, he remains the central character of an excellent comic action, and why, on the other, his relationship with Agnès must generate a psychological drama of a quite different tone. It is, therefore, appropriate to consider separately these two aspects of Molière's creation.

3

L'Ecole des Femmes:
The Laughter Machine

W̲ʜᴀᴛᴇᴠᴇʀ else it may have become, *L'Ecole des Femmes* is a fine example of the kind of comic imbroglio which requires one initial and major concession from the audience: namely, a willingness to suspend disbelief at least to the extent of accepting an arbitrary plot as the basis of an exercise in pure entertainment in the fantasy-world of the theatre. As such, it implies a certain complicity between author, actor and audience, and on the part of the author, a commitment to provide in the first instance not moral instruction or propaganda of any kind, but the gratuitous pleasure of a self-justifying art-form, whose integrity is to be judged not by reference to external values or truths, but by the logic of internal relationships in the development of the given situation.

Molière's first professional concern is, therefore, to furnish a plot which is reasonably self-contained, in that the conclusion is not incompatible with the expectations raised by the introduction. Although we are not aware of the precise manner in which this requirement will be fulfilled, nothing in the exposition suggests that the outcome of Arnolphe's scheming will be anything other than failure, or that his arrogance will result in anything but ridicule. Indeed, Molière goes out of his way to emphasize that as one who has found a "plaisir de prince" in savouring other men's marital disasters, Arnolphe is the last person who should expose himself to the risks. Again and again Chrysalde warns him, in the burlesqued overtones of heroic tragedy, that he is tempting fate, that pride will precede a fall and that he will end as a biter bit, a scoffer become laughing-stock (I, 1, vv. 45-6, 56,

66-72). However, as a purveyor of laughter, Molière has a complex task, because the pleasure of situation-comedy is not necessarily of one kind. The audience's laughter may express satisfaction at having its anticipations fulfilled, or, conversely, it may be a spontaneous reaction to sheer surprise; and such is Molière's ingenuity in this play that he has catered for both, and to such good effect that it is impossible to say that either is predominant.

The key to the operation is Molière's desire, as an efficient craftsman, to get the greatest effect out of the least material, which, as we know, has led him to make almost everything dependent on Horace's ignorance of Arnolphe's dual identity, thus creating a basic irony of situation giving rise to movements which are essentially the same, yet always new in detail; and providing the audience with both reasons for laughter. In practice, the process involves abortive initiatives by Horace and counter-measures by Arnolphe which prove equally abortive, but for different reasons at different stages: first, because he underrates the perils inherent in Agnès's naïvety; then because he makes no allowance for her intelligent and rapid reactions to realities; and finally because he is ignorant of her true identity. The net result is that once given a start, the play begins to run on like a finely-balanced machine, with alternating impulsions and occasional help from Agnès herself, to ensure a succession of complete revolutions or changes of fortune of the traditional kind.

Since Molière is more interested in mental states than in physical events themselves, most of the latter take place off-stage, usually between acts; but the process begins ten days before the raising of the curtain, when Arnolphe, confident of the success of his plans and impatient to exhibit his prospective bride to the incredulous Chrysalde, commits the fatal error of going off on some unexplained journey into the country (I, 2, v. 200). Within two days Horace has appeared, and with the aid of a classic – and marvellously narrated – "balcony scene" (II, 5, vv. 484-502) and the services of an equally classic go-between (II, 5, vv. 503-534), has insinuated himself into the household with a week to spare in which to influence Agnès. In love, even more than in politics, a week is a long time, and it enables Horace to gain, through the girl's very innocence, a psychological advantage which more than neutralises the effects of Arnolphe's twenty years of philosophising and thirteen years of experimentation. From the effects of this initiative, which coincides with the culmination of Arnolphe's hopes and premature exultation, the latter can never really recover even though the *étourderie* of Horace seems repeatedly to put him back in the lead. And it is in accordance with the system that in the coincidental exposition-scene Arnolphe receives from Chrysalde the first warning that he is tempting inexorable fate; and that by the end of the first act he has to begin the distasteful process of swallowing the bitter pills of disillusionment and frustration, although hope is kept alive by the concealment of his dual identity. So, the mechanical operation of Molière's blend of farce, *comédie d'intrigue* and burlesque produces the following *péripéties,* or reversals of fortune.

In Act I, 4, Arnolphe's glow of confident anticipation is extinguished by his first encounter with Horace, to whom he willingly gives money, only to discover that it is to be spent on thwarting that *homme bizarre* Monsieur de la Souche, and laying siege to Agnès, whose isolation has already been breached (I, 4, vv. 343-4).

In Act II, 5, Arnolphe's fears are replaced by relief at discovering that Agnès has not been seduced after all, and that he is not a pre-marital cuckold. The long-projected marriage must therefore be expedited, and will take place (as so often in Molière) "dès ce soir" (vv. 622-3). And on his next appearance, Horace is to be met not just with the physical barrier of a closed door, but with at least symbolic violence in the form of a stone, thrown from a window by a reluctant Agnès (vv. 634-640).

In Act III, 2, Arnolphe ostensibly re-establishes his ascendancy over Agnès by processes of moral tyranny, only to find on meeting Horace (III, 4) that the stone, duly thrown, has been the means of delivering to Horace a letter which Agnès's inadequately restricted education has enabled her to write, and which he must endure having read to him (III, 4, vv. 940-947).

By Act IV, 4, Arnolphe is taking the initiative, and programmes his robot-like servants to repulse the anticipated next approach by Horace; but learns from the *étourdi* himself (IV, 6) that Agnès has already secretly admitted him to the house and successfully hidden him – and proposes to do so again during the night.

With his frustration now entering into a crescendo, Arnolphe's only answer to this is actual violence; and the servants are now directed (IV, 9) to beat the young man as he climbs a ladder to Agnès's window. But this too goes wrong, for instead of receiving the carefully *prescribed* beating on his back, Horace *accidentally* falls (V, 2, vv. 1380-1385 – a beautiful "microcosmic" moment!); and being stunned, is left for dead by the dim-witted and panic-stricken servants, who communicate their panic to a demoralised Arnolphe. In the general confusion Agnès escapes to the arms of her conveniently resuscitated lover who, still believing that he is opposed by the mysterious Monsieur de la Souche, entrusts her temporarily to – Arnolphe!

At this point Arnolphe is as least physically in control, but in a climactic scene (V, 4) finally loses all hope of retaining her affections. This does not, however, mean that Horace has yet won, because Arnolphe can still return her to the convent; and Horace's own freedom of action appears to be compromised by a new development: i.e. the arrival of his father Oronte with plans to marry him to "the daughter of Enrique". So, in a last confidential speech to Arnolphe – still regarded as his friend – he asks for support against Oronte's project (V, 6), only to be betrayed by Monsieur de la Souche (V, 7). For the last time, therefore, Arnolphe has the scent of triumph, not, indeed, in his original aspirations, but in the hope of vengeance for their failure; with the prospect of consigning Agnès to her convent for ever, and helping to ensure that Horace will be married to a girl he does not want. But it turns out, with the recognition of the paternal status of Enrique and the identification of his daughter, that she is the girl whom he does want...

At the structural level of the *comédie d'intrigue,* therefore, the play has moved through half a dozen major revolutions of fortune, and Molière's only remaining problem is that of actually getting the curtain down. The answer to it is simple since, just as the movement could be prolonged indefinitely on the given basis of obscured identities, so the arbitrary revelation of true identities removes the impulsions from all sides, and the mechanism simply runs down. It is helped to do so in a purely formal dénouement consisting mostly of an exchange of couplets by Chrysalde and Oronte, the chorus-like effect of which prepares the ground for a final salute to Providence "qui fait tout pour le mieux". This dénouement (the effect of which is sometimes blurred by some omissions in actual performance) certainly seems perfunctory, and it has raised many critical eyebrows – including, sad to say, those of such an intelligent man as Voltaire – because of its alleged "artificiality"; and it has helped to propagate a myth that Molière, a recognized master of exposition, is either indifferent or incompetent in the matter of ending his plays (*6,* Pt. III, Vol. 1, p. 250). In fact, its mechanical nature is, artistically speaking, absolutely *right* for the kind of entertainment which we have been examining so far, because the actors themselves must put irony into their pronouncements, and thus reaffirm that complicity with the audience which is a requirement of the genre, by more or less laughing at themselves.

It must be added, however, that this is not quite the full conclusion of the play, because within it there is a further element that completes a quite different and much more significant drama, which Molière has developed within the framework of this sophisticated and hilarious nonsense. Although Horace is technically responsible for much of it, the essence of it is the relationship between Arnolphe and Agnès, which remains to be considered.

4

L'Ecole des Femmes: Arnolphe and Agnès – The Psychological Drama

W HEREAS the comic machine functions evenly throughout the five acts, the real and intensely personal drama is concentrated mainly in three scenes: Act II, 5; Act III, 2; and Act V, 4. They are among the longest and, structurally, the strongest; and they are particularly challenging from the performers' point of view, partly because of variations in tone, but especially because of an emotional content which has to be interpreted and controlled very carefully.

It opens with the first staged encounter between the ill-assorted pair (I, 3), which confirms the picture of the girl's innocence drawn by Arnolphe for the benefit of Chrysalde. The scene is brief, being orientated, so far as Agnès is concerned, to physical existence and physical activities. It is visual in that she appears "la besogne à la main" (v. 231), and "shocking" because of her honest allusion to the primitive truth of the existence of fleas (v. 236); but it is enough to incite Arnolphe to proffer a burlesque challenge to destiny in the name of "cette honnête et pudique ignorance" (v. 248).

But it is precisely this ignorance which is called into question by Arnolphe's first meeting with Horace, following which he feels compelled to extract from the girl her account of events during his absence, in a delicate inquisition in which, ironically, "l'examinateur souffre seul tout le mal" (vv. 565-6). The scene (II, 5) in which this is done is a dramatic masterpiece in itself, and one of Molière's very best; for in it the comic potential of an anxiety-state is exploited to the limit, as Arnolphe, alternating between fear and relief, treads delicately forward on his thin ice in an attempt to find out whether Agnès has been seduced or not, and thereafter, to put the proposition of immediate marriage. The bated breath, the exhalations of relief, the embarrassed probing for what he does not want to find, the inevitable failures of communication and the equivocal words are an object-lesson for all who may entertain doubts about the place of emotion in comedy; and most brilliant of all, perhaps, is the apparently effortless prolongation of Arnolphe's agony, as one comic trick or situation gives way to another at an appropriate relay point, to create half a dozen phases none of which could be seriously faulted. The first is the slow, awkward and tentative introduction leading to Agnès's narration, showing how Horace saw her on the balcony (that symbol of impossible mental imprisonments!) and how Arnolphe's citadel was penetrated by the time-honoured figure of the superannuated female go-between. This account, punctuated by the emotional responses of Arnolphe, is a remarkable example of the advantages which, in skilled hands, the classical *récit* can have over direct physical representation, especially with the help of that *jeu du théâtre* which is so dear to Molière.

In this case, the text has to be brought to life by Agnès's miming of an increasingly automatic succession of *révérences* (vv. 485-502), and the quoting of direct speech (vv. 512-534), to which the complement is not so much what Arnolphe says as the anguish which, too deep for words, can only be conveyed by gesture or facial expression. In this way we are made to *visualize* a past action as we *see* a present one, and to penetrate by *imagination* into the mind of Arnolphe, which is the true theatre of this drama.

As though this were not value enough in itself, there follows a second and more intense build-up and release of anguish as he probes into Horace's visits to the house, and is punished by a difficulty of communication for which he is himself responsible. This is the episode of the suggestive "le", which brings Arnolphe to a total breakdown of restraint, until his prurient mind is finally persuaded that all she has lost to Horace is a ribbon (vv. 571-580). Breathing again, he moves to re-affirm his mastery by at last broaching the subject of marriage, albeit in terms of divine sanctions and sin, for which his punishment is the *quiproquo* of the simple girl's belief that he is talking about marriage to Horace (vv. 610-627). This is the point where the impossibility of a true rapport between them leaves him no recourse but authoritarianism and, as far as Horace is concerned, violence. Agnès's reluctance to harm the youth by throwing the "grès" is met with a peremptory

Je suis maître, je parle: allez, obéissez   (v. 642)

and we would indeed be well into a *drame* were it not for the fact that this conclusion to the scene and the act is a parody of Corneille (*Sertorius,* vv. 1867-8), reminding the original audience, and us, that we are still in a world of burlesque, calling for special complicities.

Between this scene and their next encounter the stone has been thrown (with the letter), and the Notary summoned; and so Arnolphe is, as he thinks, safely re-installed in his position of mastery. This establishes most of the tone of Act III, 2, in which Molière, following the line of Scarron, has retained a set piece within his highly mobile plot. It consists of a "sermon" from Arnolphe, so finely composed according to the rhetorical conventions as to add its own dimension of burlesque and ironic parody to the basic irony of the situation; and this is reinforced by the *Maximes du Mariage* which the apparently submissive Agnès is made to read aloud. Apart from that she utters not a single word; and thus the contribution of the scene to the *drame psychologique* is, in fact, that it uses the most developed, formalized and theoretically effective mode of communication *de haut en bas* to make absolutely certain that there will be no real communication, and hence no meeting of minds. It is, in short, a scene of "eloquence" in which the most eloquent thing is the silence of Agnès; and thus Molière relies again on the *jeu du théâtre* to complete the audience's response.

Since this is not likely to be favourable to Arnolphe, it is instructive to see how the "sermon" deepens the pit into which he must fall. In fact, everything about it is wrong, from whatever point of view it is considered. First, the benefits of marriage for Agnès are presented in terms of social advancement, inauthentic in themselves and, presumably, incomprehensible to the girl. The theme of the major development

Votre sexe n'est là que pour la dépendance   (v. 699)

is equally wrong (though it might command support at the time), as is the menacing tone of the hell-fire approach, which can again hardly be comprehensible to Agnès. And since the inflated moralising of Arnolphe has to be set against our recollection of his prurient scandalmongering, it cannot but denote hypocrisy. So, by his moral bludgeoning and blackmail Arnolphe emerges more and more as a grotesque and repugnant mask-figure, and overplays his hand through vanity, and through what appears to be the confidence of a truly dominant figure, but is in fact the bluster of a man who is incapable of forming satisfactory relationships. It is significant, therefore, that he finally falls back on the sanction of religion and its rituals, for the requirements of his own ego can be satisfied with nothing less than the reduction of a wife's status and actions to "l'office de la femme" (v. 743).

The conditioning of Agnès reaches its climax, therefore, (when it is already too late) with the *Maximes du Mariage,* which lend trappings of spiritual authority to what is effectively the reduction of a human being to the status of a chattel. This is a serious moment, lightened again by a suggestion of parody; for the maxims (not all of which are totally unreasonable) have been related, rightly or wrongly, to the Institutions of St. Gregory of Nazianzen (*6,* Pt. III, Vol. 1, p. 246). However, since, according to the text, Agnès reads out ten of them (though with an indication of an eleventh to follow), they have also been associated with the Decalogue. This idea of Ten Commandments of Marriage is plausible in that Arnolphe does give a vague impression of descending from some private Sinai, but debatable in that Molière would probably shrink from such overt mockery of religion. On this point no conclusion is possible, especially as the number of maxims was soon reduced to four in actual performances.

One thing that is clear, is that this controversial scene brings the drama very close to its climax, and it requires only the matter of the letter to persuade even Arnolphe that he has failed in his major aim of possessing and shaping another human mind. It is in a state of near-despair that he utters the consecutive monologues marking the transition from Act III to Act IV: passages which not only convey all the nuances of incredulity, stupefaction, pain and indignation, injured pride and frustration, but introduce a new and seemingly genuine sentiment of love, discovered too late at a moment of the bitterest irony (III, 5, vv. 986-999). From now on it is the *jeu du théâtre* rather than the text which must be relied on to keep the relationship within the comic field; for in so far as Arnolphe begins to find words of true emotion, so he will sound more and more like the protagonist of a real rather than a burlesque tragedy. Nevertheless, at the close of Act III he is still "philosophising" about his problem, invoking the stoic "constance" of Chrysalde's burlesque exhortations (vv. 1006-7); and it is only in the last of the three great scenes with Agnès (V, 4) that he descends sufficiently from the plane of abstraction to be able to see the girl as an autonomous human being, and begin to talk to her in words which give painfully clumsy and painfully comic expression to something like love.

The significance of Act V, scene 4 is that it shows the effects of their ideas of love on both characters, and that it brings the relationship to the predictable point of a reversal of roles. In that sense it is climactic, but within the climax there are, again, various changes of position and many psychological nuances.

On Arnolphe's side the process involves the gradual and grudging abandonment of the strongpoints of his perverted rationalism; whereas Agnès, in a situation which makes sudden demands on all the resources of her newly-awakened personality, fends him off with a cool and incisive brevity (vv. 1520-1540) which leaves the erstwhile lord and master no recourse but to plead for the love which his self-centredness has made impossible. Morally, Arnolphe merits no sympathy, for, as Agnès points out, he has had every opportunity to

awaken her love (v. 1536). Age is not the barrier: Arnolphe fails
and stands condemned not because he is an old man in love
with a young girl, but because he is a middle-aged fool who, for
whatever obscure reasons, has misused the advantage of his
years to impose upon a relationship of feeling an intellectual
structure of tragi-comic incongruity. This is made manifest at
the opening of this final tête-à-tête, when Arnolphe, in genuine
astonishment at the change in Agnès from puppet to person,
attempts to hold her by an obligation of gratitude. This is an
argument from a rationalised morality which would make things
easier for *him* at a moment when there is perhaps a dawning
realisation of his own egoism; but it can make no impression on
Agnès, who can see no moral failure on her part, and in
response to further pressure can only honestly state the simple
fact that she loves Horace. In reply, Arnolphe continues to
invoke desperately the concept of "ought" (Le deviez-vous
aimer, impertinente? v. 1523), thus himself forcing Agnès to
start *arguing* for the first time in her life, and to point out that
her obligation is to Horace, for having revealed to her not what
she knows, but what it is *possible* for her to know (vv. 1562-3).
Thus Arnolphe, the philosopher and perverted idealist, is
outpointed at the first attempt by this newly-enlightened "belle
raisonneuse", whose swift insight is capable, no doubt, of un-
limited feminist developments. So a circle of intellectual comedy is closed with impeccable irony; but in closing it, Molière
returns us simultaneously to the emotional drama. Because
Arnolphe has no answer to Agnès's final point, his resentment
turns to the thought of violence (as it has done in the case of
Horace); and if the threatened blows are not struck, it is because
she offers no resistance.

AGNÈS: Hélas! vous le pouvez, si cela peut vous plaire.
ARNOLPHE: Ce mot, et ce regard, désarme ma colère...
                              (vv. 1568-1569)

This is the turning-point, and the humiliation of Arnolphe
expresses itself in a display of grotesque pleading which the
beholder can mock, or even pity, but which cannot touch the
heart of Agnès (vv. 1586-1604). So, reason and such *tendresse*

as he is capable of, having both failed him, Arnolphe has no
solid footing left, except in returning to the stance of the
tyrant; and in a last explosion of anger, he determines to send
her to the permanent prison of the convent (v. 1611).
Although this remains as a possibility until almost the end of
the play, when it is cancelled by the last, inexorable movement of Molière's "machine", he still has to find expression
within his mechanical run-down for Arnolphe's final reaction
to the catastrophe which takes Agnès out of his life and returns *him* to the prison of his thoughts. And so we have the
missing piece of the dénouement, as Arnolphe stalks off,
suffocating on precisely two interjections: *quoi!* and *ouf!* (vv.
1740, 1764), than which nothing, surely, could convey more
appropriately the incoherent chaos and frustration attendant
upon the collapse of a whole mental world – if such a thing is
to be given a *comic* expression.

It is clear even from a brief analysis of its constituent
elements why this play met with immediate success, and why
it continues to be regarded as a landmark in Molière's career.
In relation to contemporary tastes, it can be seen as an
effective entertainment-package, retaining popular features of
farce and displaying at the same time his mastery of the
techniques of the fashionable *comédies d'intrigue.* One part
of the recipe for instant appeal which has, perhaps, not been
so widely appreciated, is the burlesque element; but this is
particularly interesting as an indication that he had reflected
at length not only on comedy but on the current fashions in
tragedy. We know from the *Critique de l'Ecole des Femmes*
that he had reservations about the latter's truth to life; and he
was equally critical of the bombast which the rival actors of
the Hôtel de Bourgogne brought to their actual performances
(*7,* p. 83). This was fair game for Molière as a satirist, and his
audiences must have been aware that what they were
enjoying was in some degree a send-up of some of the more
solemn theatre of the time. This is a point to be borne in
mind whenever questions are raised about the serious aspects
of his own work; and the frequency with which they *are*
raised confirms that he wrote to make people think as well as

laugh. His ability to do so depends very much on the creation of idiosyncratic characters, of whom Arnolphe is the first outstanding example. From the obsessive follies of such characters we can certainly derive some sort of instruction, yet it is probably a mistake to regard *L'Ecole des Femmes* as essentially a work of high moral purpose. There is testimony that Molière played the character very much for laughs, and the line of moral instruction is by no means clear. In fact, different parts of the text carry different moral implications, all equally valid: for example, that we should not mock lest we be mocked; that one should not interfere with nature; or that women have rights; or that religion should not be abused; or that a little philosophy is a dangerous thing; or that marriage should be based on mutual respect. The strongest condemnation falls on selfishness; and the most positive assertion is that of the fundamental dignity of the individual, over whom no other individual has a prescriptive right of possession. Themes of this kind can lift comedy, and even buffoonery, to a new level of moral significance; but their very multiplicity, combined with complexity of characterisation, suggests that Molière is a moralist in the analytical rather than the didactic or polemical sense; and that in this play, at least, he remains predominantly an entertainer.

5

Le Misanthrope:
The Genesis of the Play

ALTHOUGH it is clearly the product of the same comic vision, *Le Misanthrope* differs from *L'Ecole des Femmes* in that it contains only one farcical scene and very little of the gratuitous fun of the *comédie d'intrigue*. On the other hand, whereas *L'Ecole des Femmes* is not conceived as a comedy of manners, this element is so prominent in *Le Misanthrope* that it seems almost more important than the character-comedy which is implied by the title. It is, in fact, a controversial work, and some of the reasons for this are suggested by the circumstances in which it was written.

It was first presented on June 4, 1666, having been composed very slowly in verse at a time when Molière was not only involved in the disputes surrounding *Tartuffe* and *Dom Juan,* but assailed by marital and medical problems. It has been suggested (e.g. by J. Cairncross in his *Molière bourgeois et libertin, 34,* pp. 68-73), that the play could have been conceived as early as 1661; but the earliest firm date for any part of the text is 1664. The question of chronology is, however, of interest in relation to an alleged autobiographical element, and to the fact that Molière modified its title. The privilege obtained in June 1666 gives a sub-title *L'Atrabilaire Amoureux,* which was subsequently suppressed. This suggests that the original conception was more broadly comic than the final version, with a relatively dispassionate presentation of a dissonant personality; and that somewhere along the way Molière's problems helped to turn it into something more like the echo of a personal drama, with serious undertones in the treatment of the central character Alceste. Although the weight of opinion is against both "autobiographical" and "tragic" interpretations, it is accepted that the play has a profoundly serious side, that it provokes smiles rather than broad laughter, and that it is deeply rooted in Molière's personal experience of life. Unlike *L'Ecole des Femmes,* it does not have the kind of plot which could be related to a specific source; and indeed, there has been argument as to whether it has an orthodox plot at all (*40,* pp. 276-292). This does not mean, however, that the subject-matter is novel, for the theme of misanthropy goes well back into antiquity, the obvious example being provided by Timon of Athens, mentioned by various writers known to Molière, including Seneca and Montaigne. And although there is no actual model for the play as a whole, it must be borne in mind that Alceste's misanthropy is related to specific social attitudes or forms of behaviour which provide important additional themes. These include the psychological theme of jealousy, the moral theme of sincerity and civility, a question of literary taste, and the broader philosophical or even religious issues raised by human imperfection. In relation to these particular matters, the source-hunters have been more successful and perhaps too successful; for the actual multiplicity of possible sources in the current of moralising literature often makes it difficult to identify the precise influences on Molière. This may be demonstrated by a single example: that of the famous theme-verses put into the mouth of Alceste's friend Philinte, whose role is to discourage over-reaction to life's imperfections:

> La parfaite raison fuit toute extrémité
> Et veut que l'on soit sage avec sobriété.
> (I, 1, vv. 151-2)

In theory these sentiments, which are central to the significance of the play, could derive from Seneca's discussion on anger in the treatise *De Ira,* either directly or through Montaigne's formula "soyez sobrement sages" (*Essais,* I, 30); but they can be related just as easily to St Paul's injunction (*Romans,* 12, 3) to every man "not to think of himself more highly than he ought to think, but to think soberly...". Suggestions as to sources for the play's ideas are, therefore, to be

treated with reserve (*40*, pp. 74-5); although a possible except-
ion is a work entitled *Prose chagrine* published in 1661 by
the philosopher La Mothe le Vayer, which is thought (e.g. by
R. Jasinski in *Molière et Le Misanthrope, 40*, pp. 261-275) to
have contributed directly to the treatment of the opposing
attitudes of indignation and resignation. But the least contest-
able of Molière's sources of inspiration are in fact his own
earlier works, of which there are various echoes in *Le
Misanthrope*. The obvious example is the adaptation in Act IV
Scenes 2 and 3 of about 150 verses from Acts II and IV of the
unsuccessful *Don Garcie de Navarre,* to add a touch of burlesque to Alceste's jealous outbursts; and there is an explicit
reference (I, 1, vv. 97-100) to the two brothers in *L'Ecole des
Maris,* as possible prototypes for Alceste and Philinte.
Following the examples of social satire in *Les Fâcheux,* the little
Impromptu de Versailles mentions a whole series of possible
characterisations including two *marquis,* a prude, a coquette,
a female wit and an *homme de qualité,* of which almost all
the characters of *Le Misanthrope* could be regarded as
realisations, except for Alceste himself. As for themes, the
question of literary taste and the opposition of a natural style
to the *faux brillants* of fashionable verse which enter into the
elaboration of the main character-study could be associated
with *Les Précieuses Ridicules*; and it is not unreasonable to
connect the theme of infidelity, brilliantly analysed in the
character of the coquette Célimène, with a similar theme in
the stopgap play *Dom Juan,* written while Molière was still
working on *Le Misanthrope* and probably worrying over the
waywardness of his wife Armande.

The discussion of influences leads, therefore, to the
conclusion that Molière worked very much from his own
resources, to produce a play of considerable originality, to
which the uncertain reaction of the first audiences may be a
testimony. The refinement of the laughter, the apparent lack
of action in favour of conversation, and the partial effacement
of the normal lines of plot-structure could be disconcerting;
and it is, consequently, worth paying close attention to the
way in which he has organized the interaction of the characters to show off his famous misfit Alceste.

6

Le Misanthrope:
The Setting and Action

THE first notable feature is the aristocratic status of all the leading characters, who are brought together as frequenters of the salon of Célimène, which replaces the more usual setting of a family circle. Célimène herself, a vivacious twenty-year-old coquette, is also a widow, this being necessary for the degree of independence which the role involves. The salon is open to all the fashionable world, represented by two empty-headed *petits marquis,* Acaste and Clitandre, and the more substantial figure of Oronte, a nobleman whose only real absurdity is his dabbling in poetry. The three of them are drawn to Célimène as moths to a candle, so becoming rivals to the principal suitor Alceste; and the group of false people is completed by Célimène's "friend", the prudish and hypocritical Arsinoé. On the other hand, the circle includes two representatives of good sense and genuine *honnêteté,* in Célimène's cousin Eliante and her friend Philinte, who is Alceste's devoted friend and confidant as well. There are also, of course, the inevitable valets, and a guard of the *Maréchaussée*; and a character not actually seen in the play – Alceste's opponent in a lawsuit, whose activities influence Alceste's own behaviour at certain key points. Between them, these characters provide a cross-section of a stratum of society with access to court-circles, and allow for permutations in relationships. Thus Célimène amuses herself by playing the field; Arsinoé simply wants a man – preferably Alceste; Eliante esteems both Alceste and Philinte; but whereas the latter is undemonstratively in love with her, Alceste is gripped by a highly demonstrative passion for the totally unsuitable Célimène.

Given these characters and circumstances, the play can hardly follow a single line of development, but advances, as it were, on a broad front with changes of emphasis in accordance not only with emotional relationships, but with peripheral matters affecting Alceste in particular. These are: a quarrel over a sonnet written by Oronte, and a lawsuit, which tend to reappear on a kind of cyclical basis, with repercussions on the main plot element, which is, of course, the impossible relationship of Alceste and Célimène. Since this scheme obviously involves some risk of fragmentation, it should be noted that Molière has provided every act with a particularly strong comic or dramatic scene, to maintain a focus of interest.

The play begins as Philinte joins Alceste, by whom he is furiously criticized for having shown excessive warmth towards a mere acquaintance. This display of disproportionate indignation over the question of civility and sincerity gets the play off to a flying start, in which, however, it is made clear that Alceste's behaviour is a malady, exposing him to ridicule (I, 1, vv. 105-6). His feelings are, in fact, generalised into expressions of hatred for humanity and its hypocrisies, exacerbated by his lawsuit, which he ought to win but is likely to lose simply because he will not follow the custom of sweetening the judges. But the major irritant is the conduct of Célimène, whose insincere charm is typical of everything that he hates, yet with whom he is illogically in love despite the fact that he is favourably regarded by both *la sincère Eliante* and *la prude Arsinoé* (I, 1, vv. 215-6). Molière thus establishes the paradox whose development will hold the play together and become a rich source of comic incongruities; and skilfully heightens Alceste's rage by having Philinte preach a totally counter-productive doctrine of moderation and indulgence towards human failings.

At this point (I, 2), the arrival of Oronte transfers the issue of civility to the plane of action, and provides a further focus for the theme of sincerity and plain dealing. Addressing an unresponsive Alceste with professions of friendship, he insists on obtaining the latter's opinion of his sonnet (which is in fact not particularly bad of its kind). From Philinte it draws

deliberately fulsome compliments, which cannot but provoke
Alceste into making a contrary response when his restraint
finally cracks. It is, however, typical of Molière's comic
subtlety that this would-be plain dealer prevaricates as long
as he can (with the famous and repeated "Je ne dis pas cela",
vv. 352, 358, 362), which suggests very early in the play that
his public stance may be masking a natural politeness.
Nevertheless, in this beautifully-managed major scene his
patience is tested to destruction, and his resulting frankness
adds a new quarrel to the frustrations he is already suffering.
So, with this classic study of loss of temper (which is one of
Molière's favourite ways of catching a character off-balance),
the act reaches a climax of its own before ending, in scene 3,
with Alceste stalking out and Philinte following in the hope
of calming him.

This is one of Molière's liveliest opening acts, orthodox in
that it introduces most of the elements of a plot, but unusual
in presenting a character in action on a minor issue, and with
little indication of what the play is really going to be about,
other than Alceste's impulses to "fuir dans un désert
l'approche des humains" (I, 1, v. 144).

In Act II the focus of interest changes, as Alceste returns
to the salon with Célimène, to give us a slightly better sense
of direction. It begins by revealing Alceste's major preoccupation: namely, the desire to apply plain speaking to the clarifi-
cation of their relationship; and, paradoxically, it indicates a
possible dénouement even though there is still no clear idea
of what sort of knot the dramatist is tying. The key
verse here is "Tôt ou tard nous romprons indubitablement"
(II, 1, v. 452), which completes the establishment of a
terminus ad quem; and the fact that it comes before Célimène
has been heard to utter a word suggests already that the
breach, if it comes, will be caused by Alceste's unyielding
temperament. His intrinsically laudable desire for sincerity is
shown again, enhanced now by his intense passion, yet also
devalued by being allied to egotism, possessiveness and
jealousy (II, 1, vv. 495-6). For it is his misfortune always to
find Célimène surrounded by admirers, whose introduction
during the rest of Act II broadens the play into a comedy of

contemporary manners, while initiating the process of frustrating Alceste's obsessive desire to have it out with Célimène and bend her to his own view of life. In scenes 2 and 3 the two marquises Acaste and Clitandre are announced, to be joined in scene 4 by the sensible Philinte and the self-effacing Eliante who, with a sulky Alceste, form an audience while Célimène and her tame marquises amuse themselves, after the fashion of the day, with satirical verbal portraits of their acquaintances.

This celebrated *scène des portraits* is the set piece of the act, serving several purposes. The gossip itself extends the range of social satire while conveying brilliantly the atmosphere of this brittle salon society; and it intensifies the scandalised exasperation of Alceste, to whose protests Célimène ripostes by sketching his own portrait (II, 4, vv. 669-680). And it is again a mark of Molière's subtlety that the "insincere" coquette is shrewd enough to state some important truths about her awkward suitor: for example, that in his plain dealing there is an *esprit contrariant* (v. 672) and a desire to be set apart from the common run of humanity (v. 675). This suggests that his elevated sentiments and contempt for frivolity conceal a certain childishness; and this is confirmed by his petulant determination to outstay the others, which points the act towards a comic conclusion. This is prolonged in the last two scenes, in which he is in fact thwarted by being summoned by the *maréchaux* to answer a complaint by Oronte over the ridiculous affair of the sonnet, which is thus brought back into the picture. The disproportion between the triviality of the matter and the rigid extremism of Alceste's attitude provides a suitably absurd ending to the act; but the frustration of his desire to deal squarely with Célimène has been further intensified.

In Act III, however, the perspective changes again, for until the last of its five scenes Alceste and his problems are removed from our gaze, and Molière is free to elaborate once more his comedy of manners, by bringing into the foreground all the characters who are the object of Alceste's high-minded contempt. In theory, this act might be difficult to fill out (as is often the case with a five-act structure), but in fact Molière has maintained the level and momentum of comedy admirably. First, it is the turn of the *petits marquis,* and in a scene of episodic satire the fashionable frivolities of their world are evoked by Acaste, in a famous self-portrait (III, 1, vv. 781-822). The balance of the scene is not, however, tilted wholly against this pair of suitors, for at the end of it they are allowed a gesture of reason, in forming a pact whereby whichever of them has the lesser chance of success with Célimène is to leave the field open for the other (III, 1, vv. 839-846). This is clearly intended to contrast favourably with the possessive jealousy of Alceste, who simply cannot conform to the rules of the adult game, but must needs claim exclusive rights to the lady.

After two linking scenes to bring Célimène back into her salon, Molière now introduces the last substantial character: Arsinoé the prude; and in scene 4 – the comic climax of the act – serves up the best single element in his social review, in the encounter of the young coquette and the frustrated older woman gnawed by jealousy. If sheer feline malice is a subject for comedy, it must be admitted that Molière has here produced an all-time classic, in which the perfidious insinuations of Arsinoé (III, 4, vv. 878-912) are adroitly and devastatingly turned against her by Célimène (vv. 913-960). This exchange, in which the *jeu du théâtre* is of the utmost importance, can be savoured as an episodic comic exercise, but it is closely integrated with the themes and atmosphere of the play. In the first place, by a typical stroke of irony, it shows the coquette doing exactly what Alceste would have her do, i.e. speaking frankly, even about Arsinoé's pathetic make-up (v. 942 – cf. I, 1, vv. 81-3); and secondly, amusing as it is, its effect on Arsinoé is to generate a degree of spite and emotion which cannot but turn the action in the direction of a *drame,* at precisely the point where the preparation of a climax is normally expected. And this expectation is justified, for as the triumphant Célimène leaves, Alceste reappears to present an obvious focus for both the desires and the resentment of Arsinoé. The act concludes, therefore (III, 5) with a movement away from the comedy of manners and back to what has gradually become the central drama of relationships, as Arsinoé penetrates Alceste's evident distaste with an offer to provide evidence of Célimène's infidelity (and a suggestion of consolation), the first of which, at least, he has not the strength to refuse.

Although a climax is clearly imminent, and one in which Alceste ceases to be entirely a *personnage ridicule*, Act IV opens quietly with a discussion between the reasonable couple Eliante and Philinte, skilfully organized to help to pull the threads of the action together and point forward to several possible developments and dénouements. First (IV, 1, vv. 1133-1162), the affair of the sonnet is almost – though not quite – disposed of, with a report that Alceste and Oronte have been partly reconciled despite Alceste's refusal to change his opinion of the poem. This allows Eliante to pronounce a much-quoted judgment of his sincerity as intrinsically *noble et héroïque* (vv. 1165-6), from which follows Philinte's repeated expression of astonishment that he should be in thrall to the unsuitable Célimène. Hence we are led to contemplate two possibilities: first, that given the uncertainty of Célimène's position, Alceste may turn to Eliante, who would probably accept him on the rebound; and secondly, that Philinte himself might happily accept Eliante on the same terms. So, Molière creates here an atmosphere of reason which is, nevertheless, also one of sensitivity and generosity, showing upper-class manners genuinely at their best. And it is to disturb this atmosphere that Alceste irrupts in scene 2, in a characteristic state of *emportement* occasioned by Arsinoé's revelation of Célimène's double-dealing, the evidence for this being a letter purportedly written by her to Oronte. It is here that Molière begins his re-use of verses from *Don Garcie de Navarre* for the burlesque exaggeration of Alceste's jealous rage and disequilibrium (e.g. IV, 3, vv. 1281-1314); but there is a sad irony as well as comedy in the scene, for Alceste does indeed offer himself now to Eliante, but with precisely the one intention – a desire for revenge – which cannot elicit a response from her delicate and prudent sensibility. Such is the clinical precision with which Molière here analyses Alceste's lack of discrimination that it is indeed difficult to say whether laughter or pity is the appropriate

response. And there is worse to come, for in scene 3 we have
at last the major confrontation between Alceste and Célimène, in which the former is as cruelly exposed as is the unhappy Arnolphe at a corresponding point in *L'Ecole des
Femmes.*

This is certainly one of Molière's most masterly scenes,
showing clearly the value of experience. It not only makes
effective use of material wasted on the unsuccessful *Don
Garcie de Navarre* but also shows him using to true dramatic
advantage the tradition of the *dépit amoureux* or lovers'
quarrel. And whereas such scenes generally contain com-
plicated movements for the purpose of light, episodic amusement, this one has a simplified structure and a central
significance; and enough emotional intensity to bring the
play up to the level of climax. It is also brilliantly ironic, for
now that Alceste has got what he wanted – the chance to
clarify his relationship with Célimène – the tension resulting
from multiple and repeated frustrations causes him to rush
into total disaster, and show himself as both ludicrous and
pitiable in his mishandling of the situation.

Being, as he says, "tout à la rage" (IV, 3, v. 1310), his
tactical error is to launch at once into an accusing and
minatory tirade, which may be technically justified but
which leaves him no reserve position if Célimène fails to
respond immediately at the same level of emotional intensity. This she presumably cannot and certainly will not do;
and consequently, by wielding a sledgehammer of criticism
and *missing,* Alceste finds himself in the classic comic position of one caught entirely off balance. Exactly in the middle
of the scene (vv. 1355-8), Célimène simply refuses to listen to
him read out the letter obtained from Arsinoé; and with her
scornful "Il ne me plaît pas, moi", in which one can almost
see the toss of the head, there begins a reversal of roles in
which Alceste, naïvely amazed at being criticized himself, is
reduced to pleading for her love, and even for a *pretence* of
fidelity (v. 1389). After trying to evade the issue, Célimène
admits that the ambiguously-worded letter is written to a
man, and specifically Oronte (v. 1365), thus conceding the
point that he has been trying to score, but forcing from him

finally a tragi-comic declaration of passion that has nothing to do with simple moral censorship, but reveals him as a pseudo-Redeemer, functioning mentally on the same kind of plane as the pseudo-Creator Arnolphe, in *L'Ecole des Femmes:*

> Ah! rien n'est comparable à mon amour extrême,
> Et, dans l'ardeur qu'il a de se montrer à tous,
> Il va jusqu'à former des souhaits contre vous.
> Oui, je voudrais qu'aucun ne vous trouvât aimable,
> Que vous fussiez réduite en un sort misérable,
> Que le Ciel, en naissant, ne vous eût donné rien,
> Que vous n'eussiez ni rang, ni naissance, ni bien,
> Afin que de mon cœur l'éclatant sacrifice
> Vous pût d'un pareil sort réparer l'injustice;
> Et que j'eusse la joie et la gloire, en ce jour,
> De vous voir tenir tout des mains de mon amour.
>
> (vv. 1422-1432)

This quite extraordinary paroxysm of passion, whose implications range from the erotic to the quasi-religious, and in which the extreme of possessiveness meets a contrary extreme of sacrifice, is certainly far removed from *la parfaite raison*. Its poignancy and sheer psychological depth also place it, arguably, well across the normal boundary of the comic; and it is for this reason that the encounter of these two non-communicating characters has to be broken off yet again. The act ends, therefore, with comic relief, in the play's only scene of farce, with Alceste in high dudgeon as his valet Du Bois *fails* to bring a letter announcing a threat of arrest following the loss of the lawsuit, which is thus re-introduced to add to the tally of Alceste's self-inflicted disasters.

In the interval between Acts IV and V three things happen to restore the sense of climax, albeit at a more rational level. Alceste now has confirmation that his suit has failed despite his belief that justice is on his side; and that his opponent has started a rumour that he, of all people, is the author of an "abominable book" (V, 1, vv. 1501-6). Worse still, the unforgiving Oronte has supported it, thus reviving all Alceste's indignation over the sonnet affair; and the combination of the two things has brought him to the decision to quit this society, conceived now in Hobbesian terms as a society of wolves (V, 1, vv. 1522-3). Philinte tries to persuade him that all is not lost, and that in respect of the lawsuit an appeal might succeed – but in vain. For twenty thousand francs Alceste will, as he sees it, have acquired the right to denounce human iniquity (V, 1, v. 1549), and he prefers his grievance to his money. In the face of this rigidity and extremism Philinte's carefully measured philosophising on the interdependence of vice and virtue is powerless. Alceste desires only to be left

> Dans ce petit coin sombre avec mon noir chagrin.
> (V, 1. v. 1584)

and only Célimène might, even at this late hour, deter him from leaving. The minor issues are now put aside, and all is set for the final dénouement, which assembles all the characters and brings back into the centre the theme of relationships, with the final exposure of Célimène. This begins in scene 2 as Oronte reappears to join Alceste in echoing the earlier arrangement between Acaste and Clitandre. Though still divided by their values (Oronte is thinking in terms of a *bonne fortune*, Alceste in terms of *le cœur* (vv. 1610-1612)), they are united in demanding that Célimène should declare her preference. As usual, she prevaricates, but this time the prevarication is undermined by Eliante, who arrives in scene 3 with Philinte to state, characteristically, that she is "pour les gens qui disent leur pensée" (V, 3, v. 1662); and it is finally defeated when Acaste, Clitandre and Arsinoé join in for the last scene.

Like most of Molière's dénouements this prolongs the uncertainties as much as possible; but whereas they usually create an atmosphere of solidarity and reassurance, this one is designed to direct a melancholy light on the unintegrated figure of Alceste. As a set piece it balances, in its first stages, the *scène des portraits* of Act II, using again the *petits marquis*, who have now discovered that the coquette's gift for portraiture has been used in letters, and turned against themselves as well as Oronte and Alceste. This time the incontrovertible evidence of the letters *is* read out by Clitandre, and the appropriate punishment indicated by the resolve of himself and his colleague to spread abroad the true portrait of Célimène's own perfidy. As they withdraw, Arsinoé makes a last play for Alceste, only to be driven out in turn by his harsh rebuff (vv. 1719-1722), leaving the defenceless Célimène to face an Alceste who, so far in this scene, has not addressed a word to her, but whose restraint seems to presage another *emportement.* This is, arguably, not a great moment of comedy, but it is certainly a great, emotionally-charged moment of theatre; and it is also a great moment of *truth,* when Célimène faces up to herself and concedes to Alceste the right to "say it all" (v. 1736) and to hate her. But while the confession of her faults completes her humiliation, it also, paradoxically, lends her a new dignity – the dignity of total honesty and penitence – apparently opening the way to that redemption which Alceste has so ardently desired for her. For a moment, therefore, there is a possibility that the couple might be able to communicate at last, for at this point Alceste – as he too confesses – has not the strength to hate her. Unhappily, however, he also lacks the capacity to respond to her confession with the absolution of pure love, which he has sought to attain; but must needs impose a *condition:* namely, that if he is to love her, she must follow him into his *désert* (vv. 1761-1768). Thus, at the last moment, he reveals himself again in the role of censor rather than redeemer, and still as an egoist and aspiring *possessor* of another human being. To this, the response of Célimène is once more one of sincerity, in the honest admission that, for her, renunciation of the world is impossible and that

> La solitude effraie une âme de vingt ans.   (v. 1774)

Nevertheless, she offers him her hand – all that she has to offer – only to be refused because it is not a heart capable of being filled by a lover. And so, in a series of *coups de théâtre* Alceste liberates himself from society, represented first by Célimène and then by Eliante, whom he also refuses, and

who by his withdrawal is made free to accept the patient
Philinte. But Alceste cannot liberate himself from his own
temperament, or from that compulsive need of self-satisfac-
tion which has attached itself to a cult of virtue so
extreme that it is simply incompatible with the compro-
mises of the world. Our last vision is of Alceste departing to
seek an *endroit écarté,* but pursued, as at the end of Act I, by
Philinte, still hoping, with the aid of Eliante, to shake his
resolve.

The play ends, therefore, in a curiously ambiguous way
with, on the one hand, the *coups de théâtre* which seem to
stress the finality of Alceste's alienation from the world, but
on the other, a movement by Philinte suggesting the
completion of a cycle. Philinte's last speech is sometimes
omitted in performances, but it is there to convey the idea
that it could all start again, with a chance that Alceste might
return when it has dawned upon him that in the backwoods
there is nobody to appreciate the actual *éclat* of his virtue,
nobody to contradict, nobody to condemn and nobody to
redeem – in short, nothing to protest about, no *raison d'être.*
This explains why the play seems to invite a sequel; and it
confirms that the action is unusual, in that it combines the
customary system of exposition, knot, climax and dénouement with a crescendo of frustration, and also with a
cyclical movement. And while it may seem to be much ado
about nothing, it takes on a much more solid appearance as
one looks more closely at the characters, and the themes
expressed through them.

Le Misanthrope:
Characters and Themes

ALTHOUGH the characters vary in importance, the first
thing to be said of them is that they all contribute to the
comedy of manners and the social satire; and it is generally
agreed that apart from its intrinsic interest and comic value
the relationship between a misanthropist and a coquette gives
Molière a splendid opportunity to say his piece about certain
elements of court-society which his personal position pre-
vented from attacking directly. The salon itself is an appropriate milieu, and Alceste's condemnations of usages and
behaviour, exaggerated though they may be, must carry some
weight as criticisms of the hypocrisy, frivolity and affectations
to be found in a particular class. Not surprisingly, therefore,
contemporary audiences sought to turn Le Misanthrope into
a pièce à clef and identify originals behind the fictional
names, with the Duc de Montausier as the model for Alceste
– unless, of course, it was the critic Boileau, or Molière
himself... These speculations (6, Pt. III, Vol. 2, p. 659; 38, pp.
184-219; 40, pp. 107-120) need not be taken too seriously,
but there is undoubtedly truth in the pictures of exaggerated
politeness, or the mania for portraits, the literary fads, or the
fashion in dress (e.g. Clitandre's "vaste rhingrave" II, 1, v.
485) or cosmetics (Arsinoé, III, 4, v. 942). The minor characters Acaste, Clitandre, Oronte and Arsinoé are there to
exemplify the lesser follies of the day; and a little of the satire
rubs off even on to the estimable Eliante, whose long speech
on the subject of love (II, 4, vv. 711-730) is a gentle send-up
of second-hand sententiousness (imitated, in fact, from Lucre-
tius, whose De rerum natura Molière had once translated).
Apart from these direct characterisations, the element of

social satire is strengthened by the atmosphere of gossip and scandalmongering in the salon, and notably, of course, in the *scène des portraits,* which allows other characters to be treated at second hand; but no more need be said of these figures, whose function is self-evident. It is otherwise, however, with Eliante, Célimène, Philinte and Alceste, who between them provide a focus for major themes going far beyond simple social satire or comedy of manners.

Of these four characters, Eliante is clearly the simplest, and perhaps the most sympathetic, esteemed by all and rightly so; and the main reason for discussing her is that with her sincerity, good sense and dignity she has been seen as Molière's "ideal woman", along with one or two other figures such as Henriette in *Les Femmes Savantes* or the older Elmire in *Tartuffe* (*38,* p. 212). This may be so, but since he did not choose to marry such a woman, it is probably more accurate to say that she represents a public norm rather than a personal preference. In the play, she is a necessary foil to both the unhappy and spiteful Arsinoé and the frivolous Célimène, and that is justification enough for the role.

Célimène, however, gives rise to more discussion, if only because she was acted by, and has been suspected of representing to some extent, the woman whom Molière did marry (*38,* pp. 201-209). In default of hard evidence, it cannot be proved that the character is in any sense a portrait of Armande; but what can be said is that she is a brilliant and credible representation of a type, and that as an autonomous *character* she has the stature to justify Alceste's love-hate response and obsession. Her role is, indeed, not much smaller than his; and at every major stage she displays complete command of the social game, whether it be in amusing her entourage with her portraits (II, 4), playing off one admirer against another or taking evasive action (IV, 3), or in pulverising Arsinoé (III, 4). And with her wit and irony, she is perceptive enough to penetrate to the weaknesses in Alceste's position, and his desire to be different, in her deftly-turned portrait of him (II, 4, vv. 669-680). She can put him on the wrong foot (II, 2, vv. 532-6, when Alceste urges her to lie, and pretend not to be at home to Acaste); and although she sometimes speaks frankly for purely tactical reasons, her final humiliation brings out a kind of intrinsic honesty which, apart from the ironic implications, suggests that she is in a sense a victim of her environment. And while she may one day become another Arsinoé, her youth and charm are conveyed so well that Alceste's feelings towards her are comprehensible, even if illogical. She illustrates both the attractions and the dangers of life in high society, and that excessive civility which is a point at issue between Alceste and Philinte who, as a pair, are responsible for much of the controversy surrounding the play, and are inextricably linked in the minds of Molière's commentators. This is inevitable, for there is certainly a special relationship between them, although it is not so easily definable as is sometimes thought.

The first point to be established from the text is that despite the close association their roles are decidedly unequal, with Philinte appearing in eleven scenes, as opposed to Alceste's seventeen. This seems to support the simplest possible interpretation of the relationship: namely, that Alceste is the *personnage ridicule* of the play and Philinte the *raisonneur,* proffering somewhat platitudinous counsels of moderation to restrain the extremism of his friend. There is obviously some truth in this view, and it fits the sort of formula to which Molière's character-comedies have too often been reduced. It also, however, tends to reduce Philinte himself to a mouthpiece for what may be, but probably is not, Molière's personal philosophy of a golden mean; and by stressing the compromiser and the conformist in him, it somehow fails to do justice to his finer qualities. which have led some critics (e.g. R. Jasinski in *Molière et Le Misanthrope, 40,* pp. 188-202) to set him up as representative of a positive ideal rather than a mere negative conformism. The simplest interpretation is also exposed to criticism from the other side, in that Alceste is by no means as ridiculous as some of Molière's other monomaniacs. His obsession is in the direction of virtue rather than vice, and he visibly suffers from the sight of forms of behaviour which are, in fact, morally questionable. It is Eliante, the play's other representative of good sense, who sums up his ambiguity in a well-known speech:

Dans ses façons d'agir il est fort singulier,
Mais j'en fais, je l'avoue, un cas particulier,
Et la sincérité dont son âme se pique
A quelque chose en soi de noble et d'héroïque.
C'est une vertu rare au siècle d'aujourd'hui,
Et je la voudrais voir partout comme chez lui.

(IV, 1, vv. 1163-8)

Although this should be taken in conjunction with Philinte's warning that his behaviour is inviting ridicule, it can be and has been drawn on to romanticize Alceste into a hero of virtue, and consequently to transform the failure of communication between him and the surrounding society into something of tragic rather than comic import (*46*, pp. 117-149). We need not, and should not accept that view; but we can agree that in so far as it is a character-comedy and not simply a comedy of manners, *Le Misanthrope* is more subtle than Molière's other productions, and calls for closer scrutiny.

As it happens, another line of enquiry is also opened up by the Alceste-Philinte relationship which, seen from another angle, is more balanced than is suggested by the actual proportion of their roles in the play. To begin with, the friendship derives not from casual encounters, but from the fact that they were actually brought up together, probably as foster-brothers. Thus Philinte:

Je ris des noirs accès où je vous envisage,
Et crois voir en nous deux, sous mêmes soins nourris,
Ces deux frères que peint l'*Ecole des maris*.

(I, 1, vv. 98-100)

This explains several things: e.g. why there is complete frankness between them; why Philinte can occasionally tease Alceste (as in Act I scene 2); why the relationship tends to express itself in terms of something like philosophical dialectic; and why, even at the end, Philinte cannot let go (and why the omission in performance of his last two lines is a betrayal of Molière's intentions). The relationship is therefore quasi-fraternal; but philosophically they are *frères ennemis*, and they do not share a family temperament, being at that level also totally opposed to each other (*40*, pp. 124-131).

This fact alone must send us back to the genesis of the play, and to the original sub-title *L'Atrabilaire Amoureux*; and it strengthens the probability that Molière's conception evolved considerably during the long process of composition. All the signs are that *Le Misanthrope* began as a comedy of *humours,* based on the traditional – if fanciful – physiology which linked temperaments to the four principal body-fluids: blood, phlegm, bile and melancholy ("black bile"); and this conception has certainly survived in the play as part of the explanation of the unsociable Alceste. But it has also survived in Philinte, who characterises himself explicitly as a cool "phlegmatic", and is criticized as such by Alceste:

PHILINTE: Mon flegme est philosophe autant que votre bile.
ALCESTE: Mais ce flegme, monsieur, qui raisonne si bien,
            Ce flegme pourra-t-il ne s'échauffer de rien?
                                            (I, 1, vv. 166-8)

This confirms that Molière had in mind some kind of balance in his presentation of two temperamental reactions to life; and if the play had remained at that conceptual level, it could be argued that he did not intend to associate himself with either attitude. It also confirms that Philinte is more than a routine *raisonneur,* and it suggests that a lot of Molière has gone into both characters.

The really interesting questions which now arise are why and how Molière moved beyond his original conception to produce the play in its final form, and to the first of them, at least, the answer is fairly simple: namely, that to a dramatist with his obvious interest in moral analysis or moral instruction, the theory of humours leads ultimately to an impasse. By reducing human behaviour to a pattern of physiological determinism, it removes the element of choice which creates the "morality" or otherwise of men's actions; and – equally important for Molière – it also removes most of the justification for ridicule, since it would imply that moral correction is

as impossible as the correction of a physical deformity.
Above all, however, he seems to have rejected the simple idea
of *l'atrabilaire amoureux* because it does not cater for all the
subtleties of either social satire or individual psychology
which he wished to incorporate in his play. Aspects of the
former have already been seen fairly clearly, and most of the
latter involve Alceste; but a number of further observations
can now be made on Philinte, and notably that in the full
development of his role he seems genuinely to represent a
superior *sagesse,* and not merely a negative and false *honnêteté,* as was claimed during the eighteenth century by the
philosopher Rousseau, in his *Lettre sur les Spectacles.*

The reason for such misunderstandings is that some of the
things which Philinte actually says do sound like platitudes of
complacency; but he is to be judged not so much by what he
says as by what he does; and above all by his quite unselfish
devotion to Alceste. To save his friend from a disastrous
entanglement with Célimène, he is willing to encourage a
marriage between Alceste and Eliante, even though it would
destroy his own quiet hopes of happiness; and while this
might be interpreted as an extreme manifestation of a "phlegmatic" philosophy, his ultimate union with *la sincère Eliante*
is surely Molière's way of rewarding, not an empty *raisonneur,* but a truly fine character who is even more aware than
Alceste of the evils in human nature, but who has learned to
live with them and do good without self-advertisement and
éclat. He is, in short, a genuine altruist, but also a realist and,
as he says:

> ... pas plus offensé
> De voir un home fourbe, injuste, intéressé
> Que de voir des vautours affamés de carnage,
> Des singes malfaisants et des loups pleins de rage.
> (I, 1, vv. 175-8)

His realism is, in effect, Alceste's lifeline – and it is still being
offered as the curtain falls, and when, having reached his own
happy ending, he could well disclaim any further responsibil-
ity for his friend.

If Philinte is the realist, Alceste is undoubtedly an idealist, but of a dubious kind. Temperamentally, he is the compulsive *protester;* but as a thinker he displays the deadly seriousness of the fanatic, the capacity to follow a line of "reason" beyond the limits of practical sense. At his worst, he is of the same breed as Arnolphe; but he is not always at his worst, and it is not for nothing that he is esteemed by the most discerning of his companions. He is, of course, a gentleman, but his precise status within his class has been a subject of debate. The fact that he is a misfit in salon society does not call into question his social standing as such; but his unfashionable literary taste (I, 2, v. 392 ff.), his brusque manner and strong language seem to be the marks of a provincial, and explain why Célimène tends to treat him as an exhibit rather than a person. His dress (the famous *rubans verts* mentioned in Célimène's letter: V, 4), has also been regarded traditionally as soberly unfashionable (*4,* p. 136; *38,* p. 157), but this interpretation is now contested *(41).* Nevertheless, the weight of evidence still suggests that an inferiority-complex is a factor in Alceste's aggressiveness, although Molière was probably more concerned to depict comic incongruities. There are, in short, social nuances which are not easily grasped nowadays, but which remind us that Molière was presenting "les gens de son siècle", and that Alceste, who is a major instrument of social satire, is himself a victim of it, albeit in a relatively mild degree.

But the satire, in the case of Alceste, is above all a moral satire, and it is here that Molière has built substantially upon the original comedy of humours, while keeping the essential basis of the *atrabilaire amoureux,* which is useful first as a psychological incongruity in itself, and secondly because the temperamental lack of control creates exaggerated effects serving the cause of both comic disproportion and the *optique du théâtre* in general.

At the moral level proper the case of Alceste is particularly interesting because it associates idiosyncrasy with good intentions, and sets up the paradox that virtue can be harmful. It is not, however, unique, since good intentions of a sort enter into the motivations of many of Molière's characters, including even the egregious Arnolphe. With Alceste, the virtue is not in question, and the willingness to confront society may be thought admirable, as we can see from Eliante's use of the term *héroïque*. But remembering what Molière said about heroes and men in Scene 6 of his *Critique de l'Ecole des Femmes,* it can be argued that for him the word *héroïque* is at best double-edged in its implications, and at worst almost pejorative, suggesting that the hero is unnatural, existing outside the bounds of normal rationality. This tallies, of course, with Philinte's criticism of his friend in the name of "perfect reason"; for Alceste does follow a line of reason, as well as his temperamental propensities, in arriving at extreme positions. This is what exposes him to ridicule, for although his *emportements* are due in part to an instability which he cannot help and which it would be "cruel" to mock, they also take him to a point where he *wilfully* defies all inducements to compromise, and sets himself above the common run of humanity, as one charged with the mission of challenging and changing the race. This wilfulness is clearly signalled in the opening scene:

Moi, je veux me fâcher, et ne veux point entendre.   (v. 5)
Je veux qu'on soit sincère ...   (v. 35)
Je veux qu'on me distingue ...   (v. 63)
Je veux que l'on soit homme ...   (v. 69)

and although his commitment to virtue may be admirable in itself as a sign of superiority, the conscious wilfulness is more that of a child than an adult, and reduces him in fact to a status of inferiority. The choleric temperament and the dedication to principle combine, therefore, to create an inflexibility which cannot mesh with the realities of life, so that his world remains egocentric and his relations with others manifestly perverted. He must either dominate or flee, and the play does of course cater for both these possibilities. And if he cannot dominate and regenerate society, he can only fall back on Célimène, whom he seeks to possess as surely as Arnolphe seeks to possess Agnès in *L'Ecole des Femmes,* even at the cost of pleading for a contractual *pretence* of fidelity (IV, 3, vv. 1389-90), and the sacrifice of his personal pride.

The fact is that in his relations with Célimène, Alceste is completely disorientated; and one can understand why his desperate attempts to rationalize his position assume more and more importance in the play. His confusion is indicated in the first scene, where he talks of his love in "rational" terms of reciprocity (v. 237), but also sees it as a weakness which can only be justified if he can "purge Célimène's soul" (vv. 233-4). And the climax of his confusion – and his need – comes, of course, in the remarkable outpouring at the end of Act IV, scene 3, where his anguished plea for the reassurance of reciprocity and possession is again caught up with a re-demptive conception of love, to justify all Philinte's mis-givings about the dangerous combination of idealism and instability in his friend.

It cannot be denied that in this scene and elsewhere there is serious psychological analysis, and genuine pathos for those who have eyes to see it; yet, looking at the scene and the play in their totality, it is difficult to resist the conclusion that ultimately we are dealing with a burlesque hero rather than the true hero dear to romantically-minded commenta-tors from Rousseau onwards. If we are not immediately aware of this, it is because Molière has replaced the broader carica-tural strokes of his picture of Arnolphe, for example, with a much more subtle manipulation of our sympathies, made possible largely by the salon background into which the char-acter-comedy is carefully blended to produce a play which by its very nature must offer a perpetual challenge to critics and producers alike.

By way of summing-up, it must be conceded that this is not Molière's "funniest" play, nor the most dramatic. What sets it apart is the fine grain of the amusement, which – in the much-quoted judgment of Molière's contemporary Donneau de Visé – "fait rire dans l'âme". It sometimes seems, in fact, to be less significant as an exercise in ridicule directed at this or that specific character or foible, than as a wry comment on the perversity of life. itself, and that obscure chemistry which determines temperaments, and such incongruous attractions as that of a Célimène for an Alceste. It was certainly meant to amuse; but since it is public property one need hardly be surprised that its ambivalence and universality have tempted actors from Lucien Guitry onwards into near-tragic interpretations of "l'homme aux rubans verts", and producers into experiments with modern dress. Even their failures are a tribute to Molière's success.

Conclusion:
Some Problems of Criticism

While *L'Ecole des Femmes* and *Le Misanthrope* represent only a part of Molière's range, they are deep enough to raise a number of general questions which have a bearing on his work as a whole, and which it is appropriate to discuss in a wider perspective.

The first of them is, rather obviously, that of the seriousness of this public entertainer; and it can be answered at several levels. First, Molière himself took his art very seriously indeed, not only at the purely technical level, but as one who apparently believed that laughter has a therapeutic or corrective function corresponding, presumably, to the cathartic or purgative effect attributed to tragedy by Aristotelian doctrine. As a satirist, he is seriously concerned by behavioural problems associated with hypocrisy, obscurantism, excessive enthusiasm or sheer stupidity; but it is doubtful whether he sees the correction as going beyond a check on the most socially damaging manifestations of folly. He had no more hope than his Philinte of changing human nature in itself, and it is a matter of notoriety that the cranks depicted in his plays are themselves not cured, though they serve as a warning to others. In this respect, it is possible that the theory of humours is relevant to other works besides *Le Misanthrope*. Secondly, as a great experimental artist, he naturally pursued his comic vision to the limit; and if he seems at times to be crossing into the territory of tragedy, this is mainly because the commitment of his central character is pushed to a point where it must generate strong emotion as well as peculiar behaviour, and quite possibly an emotional response to that emotion. Consequently, those who share the view of Horace Walpole that "this world is a comedy to those that think, a tragedy to those that feel" will not be surprised that, for some, a case such as that of the misfit Alceste has a tragic resonance about it. It should also be remembered that while Molière obviously did not set out to write tragedies in disguise, the dramatic standards which he was emulating had in fact been set in the field of tragedy; and that the most successful tragedies, during most of his career, were the so-called heroic tragedies of Corneille, in which the protagonists were distinguished by their total commitment to some principle or personal value, and hence to a line of conduct. The fact that Molière occasionally parodies Corneille suggests that it is not entirely fanciful to postulate a burlesque relationship between the *jusqu'auboutisme* of the tragic Cornelians and the pig-headedness of those Molière characters whose own obsessive seriousness renders them impenetrable to reason and advice, and hence literally *absurd* in the strict senses of that abused word – i.e. dissonant or totally deaf.

To the related question of whether Molière really has or expects any sympathy for his great eccentrics, the answer seems to be that it depends on the relative seriousness of the antisocial consequences of the eccentricity. Alceste is treated more sympathetically than Arnolphe, and there are some comparable characters such as Jourdain, the *Bourgeois Gentilhomme,* whose foible – snobbery – is so commonplace that it can be treated lightly in a spirit of fun and pure entertainment. As a thinking man, Molière probably becomes more compassionate as he realises that there are reasons for eccentricity, and that apart from one thing a man may be perfectly respectable and normal.

Over the years there has been debate as to Molière's position with regard to the social organization of his time, and whether his plays are written from the standpoint of a particular class (*3*, pp. 159-181; *33*). This question arises inevitably from the ambiguity of his own situation as a court-entertainer of bourgeois origin. Between them, *L'Ecole des Femmes* and *Le Misanthrope* suggest that he was not a class-orientated propagandist, but a *moraliste* passionately interested in all sorts and conditions of men and women. In the one, he puts a bourgeois into the pillory, in the other a whole set of aristocrats. Elsewhere, he illustrates both the ignorance and the shrewdness of the lower orders; and in *Dom Juan* he points out very clearly that one can be a *grand seigneur* but a *méchant homme*. On the face of it, therefore, arguments about his social orientation seem rather pointless, but they do have some bearing on the broader issues of morality and philosophy which enter into his preoccupations.

Although Molière was subjected to accusations of dubious morality – for example, in the case of *L'Ecole des Femmes* – his defence was that immorality is in the eye of the beholder. No doubt this can be seen as special pleading, but it must be remembered that the theatre as a whole, and the acting profession, were exposed to the charge of being an *école de mauvaises mœurs,* especially on the part of the more prejudiced religious groups; and that this attitude was to be maintained for a long time by those who seem to have forgotten the ancient historical links between drama and religion. In fact his plays, considered as a whole, maintain a remarkably healthy tone, with little crudity and no sniggers, but much and consistent defence of social order, family solidarity, the dignity of individuals, including women and children, and a genuine hatred of the corrosive power of hypocrisy and selfishness. Despite his frequent mockery of bourgeois characters he has been seen, especially by nineteenth-century critics, as fundamentally a defender of "middle-class morality" – a point which naturally leads into the question of his so-called philosophy.

Molière's "philosophy" is something of a pitfall, mainly because it tends to be seen in terms of the pronouncements of the *raisonneurs* who appear so regularly in his plays, to establish principles of moderation and common-sense, or conformity to nature or the golden mean. "La parfaite raison fuit toute extrémité" may be a defensible proposition in the mouth of a Philinte; but figures such as Chrysalde are a little more ambiguous, reminding us that the *raisonneurs* themselves may be the object of gentle satire, and that their sententiousness is sometimes a little tongue-in-cheek. The point is that the conformist, moderate and essentially *prudent* views even of the straightforward *raisonneurs* are part of the stock-in-trade not of a philosopher, but of a comic playwright whose aim is to entertain and, on the whole, reassure his audience; and the obvious corollary to this is that Molière himself does not appear to have lived according to these public precepts, but took risks – the risks of an uncertain profession, the risk of marrying a young girl – anything but the risk of mediocrity, however golden.

Finally, there is the related question of Molière's religious position, which first arises with *L'Ecole des Femmes*, although it does not explicitly concern *Le Misanthrope*. On this matter there is a division of opinion between those who see him as an anti-Christian *libertin* and forerunner of the eighteenth-century *philosophes (34),* and those who accept his assurances that he was opposed not to religion, but to the abuses and perversions of religion. He certainly disliked, satirized and offended many religious people, particularly with *Tartuffe* (although the atheist Dom Juan comes, of course, to a bad end); and privately, at least, he may have entertained serious doubts; but even so his work shows the pervasive influence of Christian thought, particularly in the ambiguity which characterises his view of human nature. Philinte, for example, sees corruption and perversity as inescapable facts of life, and his major characterisations, with their paradoxical mingling of idealism and folly, and fatal flaws of selfishness (as seen in both Arnolphe and Alceste) are not very different from the visions of those contemporary Christian moralists such as Pascal, who accepted as a matter of course the implications of Original Sin, and shared the stereoscopic view which enabled Molière to "peindre d'après nature" and create characters of depth and human complexity.

Bibliographical Note

Since there is a vast critical literature on Molière, the following list is merely representative of what is useful and reasonably accessible, mainly among modern publications.

I. BACKGROUND AND GENERAL

1. Adam, Antoine, *Histoire de la littérature française au XVIIe siècle*, Paris, Domat, 1952 (in particular, Vol. 3).
2. Attinger, G., *L'Esprit de la commedia dell'arte dans le théâtre français*, Neuchâtel, La Baconnière, 1950.
3. Bénichou, Paul, *Morales du Grand Siècle*, Paris, Gallimard, 1948. A very important chapter on Molière.
4. Brereton, Geoffrey, *French Comic Drama from the Sixteenth to the Eighteenth Century*, London, Methuen, 1977.
5. Gossman, L., *Men and Masks*, Baltimore, Johns Hopkins U.P., 1963.
6. Lancaster, H.C., *A History of French Dramatic Literature in the XVIIth Century*, 10 vols, Baltimore, Johns Hopkins U.P., 1929-1942 (in particular, Part III, in two vols). Indispensable background material.
7. Moore. W.G., *The Classical Drama of France*, Oxford U. P., 1971.
8. Scherer, Jacques, *La Dramaturgie classique en France*, Paris, Nisard, 1950. Essential guide to dramatic techniques of the period.

II. MODERN EDITIONS OF MOLIÈRE

9. *Œuvres Complètes* (Les Grands Ecrivains de France), Paris, Hachette, 1873-1901.
10. *Œuvres Complètes* (Bibl. de la Pléiade), ed. M. Rat. 2 vols, Paris, Gallimard, 1933.
11. *Théâtre Choisi*, ed. M. Rat, Paris, Garnier, 1963. Including *L'Ecole des Femmes* and *Le Misanthrope*.
12. *Œuvres Complètes*, ed. R. Bray, Paris, Les Belles Lettres, 1933-1952.
13. *Œuvres Complètes*, ed. R. Bray and J. Scherer, Paris, Club du Meilleur Livre, 1954-1956. Useful on theatrical and farce aspects.
14. *Œuvres Complètes* (Coll. L'Intégrale), Paris, Eds du Seuil, 1962.
15. *Œuvres Complètes* (Bibl. de la Pléiade), ed. G. Couton, 2 vols, Paris, Gallimard, 1971. Replaced the Rat edition of 1933.
16. *L'Ecole des Femmes* (Classiques Larousse), ed. J. Bénazéraf, Paris, Larousse, 1990.

17. *Le Misanthrope* (Classiques Larousse), ed. G. Gengembre, Paris, Larousse, 1990.

18. *L'Ecole des Femmes* (Les Classiques de la Civilisation Française), ed. D. Justum, Paris, Didier, 1977. Very *scolaire*, but contains useful material and illustrations.

NOTE: since not all editions give numbered lines for the verse comedies, these *éditions scolaires* are still convenient working texts, despite limitations.

III.   BIOGRAPHIES

19. Grimarest, *Vie de Monsieur de Molière*, Paris, 1705.
    Modern edition: Paris, La Renaissance du Livre, 1930.
20. Fernandez, Ramon, *La Vie de Molière*, Paris, Gallimard, 1930.
21. Brisson, Pierre, *Molière, sa vie dans ses œuvres*, Paris, Gallimard, 1942.
22. Mongrédien, Georges, *La Vie privée de Molière*, Paris, Hachette, 1950.
23. Simon, Alfred, *Molière par lui-même* (Coll. Ecrivains de Toujours), Paris, Eds du Seuil, 1957, 1976. A useful introduction, laying some emphasis on the allegedly subjective element in Molière's works.
24. Chevalley, Sylvie, *Molière en son temps 1622-1673*, Paris/Geneva, Minkoff, 1973.

IV.   STUDIES

25-27. Michaut, Gustave, *Jeunesse de Molière; Les Débuts de Molière à Paris; Les Luttes de Molière*, 3 vols, Paris, Hachette, 1923-1925. Still a standard work, though dated in parts.
28. Mornet, Daniel, *Molière, l'homme et l'œuvre*, Paris, Hatier-Boivin, 1943.
29. Moore, W.G., *Molière, a new criticism*, Oxford U.P., 1949. A short but stimulating study, from the inside.
30. Audiberti, J., *Molière dramaturge*, Paris, Eds de l'Arche, 1954.
31. Bray, René, *Molière, homme de théâtre*, Paris, Mercure de France, 1954.
32. Cairncross, John, *New Light on Molière*, Geneva, Droz, 1956.
33. Descotes, Maurice, *Les Grands Rôles du théâtre de Molière*, Paris, P.U.F., 1960.
34. Cairncross, John, *Molière bourgeois et libertin*, Paris, Nizet, 1963. A strong thesis, as the title suggests.
35. Guicharnaud, Jacques, *Molière, une aventure théâtrale*, Paris, Gallimard, 1963. One of the most important studies in recent years. Valuable for *Le Misanthrope*, but does not deal with *L'Ecole des Femmes*.
36. Hubert, J.D., *Molière and the Comedy of Intellect*, Berkeley, University of California Press, 1967.
37. Jasinski, René, *Molière*, Paris, Hatier, 1969.
38. Doumic, René, *Le Misanthrope de Molière*, Paris, Eds Mellottée, 1929.
39. Arnavon, Jacques, *Le Misanthrope de Molière*, Paris, Plon, 1946.

40. Jasinski, René, *Molière et Le Misanthrope,* Paris, Colin, 1951. A very important though somewhat controversial study. Stresses the subjective element, and the importance of the character of Philinte.
41. Lawrenson, T.E., 'The Wearing o'the Green' in *Molière: Stage and Study. Essays in Honour of W.G. Moore,* Oxford U.P., 1973.
42. Wadsworth, P.A., *Molière and the Italian Theatrical Tradition.* York, S. Carolina, French Lit. Publications Company, 1977.
43. Howarth, W. D., *Molière: a Playwright and his Audience,* C.U.P., 1982.
44. Peacock, N., *Molière. L'Ecole des Femmes,* University of Glasgow French and German Publications, 1988.
45. Whitton, D., *Molière. Le Misanthrope,* University of Glasgow French and German Publications, 1991.

V. MISCELLANEOUS

46. Collinet, Jean-Pierre, *Lectures de Molière,* Paris, Colin, 1974. A guide to critical opinions and changing attitudes to Molière over three centuries, with a valuable bibliographical appendix.
47. Rousseau, Jean-Jacques, *Lettre à D'Alembert sur les spectacles,* 1758. Contains the famous criticism of *Le Misanthrope,* largely responsible for the "romantic" interpretations of Alceste.
48. Bergson, Henri, *Le Rire. Essai sur la signification du comique,* 1900. The philosopher's constantly reprinted classic on the subject. Still relevant to certain aspects of Molière, though obviously not the last word.

CRITICAL GUIDES TO FRENCH TEXTS

edited by
Roger Little, Wolfgang van Emden, David Williams